A History of Indian Advertising in Ten-and-a-Half Chapters*

*(Or Stark Raving Ad)

Ritu Singh has been an ad-crafter for many years now, and has worked with J. Walter Thompson (JWT) India and the Times of India group. Early on in her career, she believed that clients were a villainous lot who lived to reject her perfect, efficient ads for their products. So, when she switched sides and became part of a marketing team, she was surprised to find that clients were, in fact, regular human beings with deep concerns about, among other things, how best to sell their products.

Being on both sides of the table has given her not only double the perspective, but also the dubiously thrilling feeling of being a double agent of sorts. In this book, she attempts to explore a third perspective on why our ads say the things they do. (No actual secret agents from the ad industry were harmed in its writing.)

Praise for the Book

'Ritu Singh...brings all this [information] out in this extraordinarily detailed but lucid presentation of a century and more of Indian advertising, with the account garnished well with a dry, wry, and quite subversive (at times) wit.' – *Hindustan Times*

'A fun tour of the Indian advertising landscape, exploring how ads are both business solutions and an entertaining facet of our lives.' – *Asian Age*

'The book is a breezy, rib-tickling and irreverent social and business history primarily of liberalized India.' – *The Hindu BusinessLine*

'The book touches upon almost all facets of Indian advertising with a fair amount of success... The author [writes] with great skill, building great atmospherics in every theme and chapter. Overall, the book makes for an interesting leisure read, but students and young marketing professionals would do well to have a copy on their shelves.' – *Tribune*

A History of Indian Advertising in Ten-and-a-Half Chapters*

*(Or Stark Raving Ad)

RITU SINGH

hachette INDIA

First published in 2018 as *Stark Raving Ad: A Giddy Guide to Indian Ads You Love (Or Hate)* by Hachette India
(Registered name: Hachette Book Publishing India Pvt. Ltd)
An Hachette UK company
www.hachetteindia.com

This edition published in 2021

1

ISBN 978-93-91028-55-8

Hachette Book Publishing India Pvt. Ltd
4th & 5th Floors, Corporate Centre,
Plot No. 94, Sector 44, Gurugram – 122003, India

Typeset in High Tower Text 11.5/15.4
by Manmohan Kumar, Delhi

Printed and bound in India
by Manipal Technologies Limited, Manipal

Contents

Premumble

Like thousands of advertising hatchlings, I was quite clueless on my first day at work in an ad agency. As I entered the office, nothing could take away from the All-Ye-Who-Enter-These-Hallowed-Portals-of-Advertising chant in my head – not the piglets scuffling through the bullshit at the entrance, not the snot-pickers near the shady (very shady) park across the road, not the absence of any team member till eleven in the morning. No, not even the sight at lunchtime of a senior copywriter wiping his hands on a newspaper after a sumptuous meal of mutton curry and rice eaten with five fine-dining tools.

I felt privileged when my creative supervisor sat me down in his gas chamber-like cabin, filled with cigarette smoke and his smoker buddies (not all offices were No Smoking zones then). He started with the Talk. 'Advertising is a complex business where you have to slog your b**t off to come up with f***ing great communication. But there is an almost magical formula for coming up with ideas. Today, I will share that with you.'

I listened reverentially as he spoke. 'Great ideas are autobiographical. A really great guy (not me) once said this: Look at the oyster – its autobiography is the pearl. So when you work, go ahead, pull out those insights from your own experiences.'

He leaned forward to make another revelation. Eager to learn more magic formulae, so did I. 'And always remember,' he said, 'every person who has made it big here has at least one divorce behind him or her.'

And that is how agency lessons/conversations have always been – the real mixed with the comic, the truth with the farcical. So it was some decades ago. And so it is now.

Whether you are part of advertising and marketing or are looking in from the outside, chances are ads have contributed to your life in some way. Maybe you finally own an anti-dandruff shampoo. Or maybe you now enter house-warming parties, one eyebrow lifted, saying, '*Wah* Sunil Babu, *naya ghar...*'

Such contribution to our betterment and such take-aways need to be documented. But the Indian advertising landscape is so vast, much of the imagery so memorable, the 30-second-duhs so many and the big ideas so fascinating that you could have a tome if someone wrote about it all.

Or you could have a giddy guide. A whistle-stop tour replete with commercials, brands, wars, characters, scandals, insights and other such stuff. All (almost) made in India. And at the heart of it all, business solutions in the guise of disruptive or, at the very least, noticeable communication. After all, ultimately, ads are about businesses feeling needy. Yes, brands need your love (and while you are at it, your wallet too, please).

The selections here are intuitive and open-ended. There are some major case studies and some minor ones. There are brand and ad mentions as well as some trivia.

Take your pick. Sift for the stuff that makes sense and enjoy the nonsense.

A little bird tells me...

Before we go any further, let's grab the massive opportunity social media gives us. Here is a peep into the posts of business heads, creative directors and brand planners. This is what the finest minds in marketing and advertising are thinking and posting on online platforms right now...

- *Sitting in a bar. And can't help but wonder how many farts are trapped in this cushion?*
- *Twain said, 'It's not the size of the dog in the fight, it's the size of the fight in the dog.' But at the end of the day, you are a dog, right?*
- *The client's brief is to set the Ganges on fire. And, of course, the brand has no money to light more than a matchstick.*
- *What kind of artist am I – always creating Cover Your A*s ad layouts for potato chips?*
- *Are most brand conversations happening offline, at the pub? Hmm, need a beer.*
- Junglee Jawaani *is running to a packed house in Rahul Talkies. Maybe watching it will give me insights into* that *audience's preferences.*

The Very First Apple Ad

THE EVE OF ADVERTISING

Advertising has always been a way of life. Whenever something has needed selling, it has relied on some form of advertising.

Advertising practitioners are quite fond of a poem about a hen and a fish. No sooner does the hen lay her egg than there is such a *cock-a-doodle-doo* that the whole world wakes up to the achievement. Meanwhile, the codfish goes about its business of laying thousands of eggs. Quietly. And no one ever hears of it.

Yes, nothing turns heads like some good old-fashioned screaming from the rooftops. But only if you like omelettes will you pay attention to all that clucking about eggs. Because, while grabbing attention may be vital, a product's relevance to the audience is even more so.

Sometimes, though, the journey from irrelevance to complete relevance can be achieved with a dollop of persuasion. In fact, that's how a transaction of biblical proportions took place.

In the Garden of Eden, the serpent knew he had limited personal charm as far as Adam was concerned. Putting together a very clever strategy, he slithered up to Eve and convinced her of the benefits of a big, shiny red apple. Convinced, she went to work on Adam. And that is how Adam got persuaded into biting the forbidden apple that he neither wanted nor needed. He paid the price for his greed...but that's another story.

Diamonds, for example, are probably way up there on any list of things that people do not need. Yet, once those crystallized carbon stones were discovered, it was not long before people took a shine to them. Lots of oh-honey-such-a-big-diamond-for-me-I-love-you-so-much exchanges later, a diamond became the official bedrock for every wedding and many a bedding.

But it took the De Beers' marketing and advertising team to show the way forward to every English magazine reader in the world. After years of seeing their ads, today we all know that spouses may come and go but 'a diamond is forever.'

Such BIG ideas are what every business believes it needs to unlock its potential. These lie in a zone that is more science than art and their hallmarks are debatably simple – stand out in the clutter, engage your consumer and never lose sight of the insight. The ultimate test of a big idea, though, is one everyone agrees on – it's got to sell.

So how do you sell to the Indian consumer?

We Indians are not exactly easy to decipher. A non-Indian could look at us and see a homogenous mix of people, all brown (despite the application of copious amounts of Fair and Lovely) but an immigration desk in another country is probably the only place where we are wholeheartedly, completely 'Indian'. In our own country, however, we are no longer merely from India – we are Bungaalis, Panjaabis, Biharis, UP-walahs and so on. The state we belong to says a lot about us...

...as do our names. In the old days, a person's name was the first clue to his or her caste and, therefore, their standing in the social hierarchy. These days, the hierarchy is not as rigid and you often find people rioting to get themselves deemed as 'lower caste'. Or, at the very least, backward.

We are not like the people from the West, we are fond of saying. Yet, corrupted by the 'West' (or maybe the 'Oriental East'), our boys eat foreign food like chowmein and some of our learned elders tell us that this is the reason why some of them rape. (No matter that our chowmein is as Indian as can be, often made with paneer and *elaichi* in it.)

We are the world's largest democracy. And sometimes our panchayats issue death sentences.

We can arrange love marriages. And we can construct futuristic buildings on roads that a bullock would refuse to pull its cart over.

We are all about IT. Why, for years we have been receiving and forwarding messages like this one: 'Send this message to 10 people right now and the Dalai Lama will grant all your wishes. For each forward, Bill Gates and Apple Inc. will donate money to research that will free the world of terrorism and Delhi of its politicians. Something terrible will happen to you if you do not forward this. Forward now!'

So, yes, this whole viral marketing thing? Indians have been practising it for years.

All of this brings us to a truism: India is as diverse a country as there can be.

It's a lesson every marketer learns in his/her diaper years: This country has many peculiarities and, therefore, poses many unique marketing challenges.

How do you sell expensive sports shoes in a country that considers them lounge accessories? How do you get people to visit your restaurant to make a meal of a pizza when they think it's a snack? How do you sell a premium detergent to Hema, Rekha, Jaya and Sushma who are dancing to the tune of a low-priced one? What will make amma get into the habit of using a liquid hand-wash instead of just bar-soaping it up?

In general, we are tough with people we are buying things from. No *ji*, we don't roll over and wag our tails when the MNCs come out to play with us. (Or even the *lala*s for that matter.) They need to kindly adjust to our ways. So, from an international chain of iconic beef burgers comes the McAloo Tikki Burger, a uniquely Indian solution for the vegetarian Indian. And the world may be eating at that joint with all the fried chicken but what's *kukkad-shukkad* without a little *masala*? We will only settle for a fiery grilled or tandoori chicken equivalent, thank you very much.

A ham and cheese pizza may be a safe bet anywhere in the world; in India, though, the dish has had to reinvent itself into a *chicken tikka* pizza in the north and the no-onion, no-garlic Jain pizza in the west.

The vastness of the land, combined with the distinct identities of every region and their inherent sociocultural nuances, can be a nightmare to decipher. For the marketer, it can be about striking it lucky on the first try. Or it can take years of research and hits-and-misses. Or it may require consumer-centric product innovations that are strategically branded and smartly positioned. And, sometimes, it can take all of the above and more.

The cliché of the unique Indian exists for a reason.

It's a lesson every marketer learns in his/her diaper years: This country has many peculiarities and, therefore, poses many unique marketing challenges.

How do you sell expensive sports shoes in a country that considers them lounge accessories? How do you get people to visit your restaurant to make a meal of a pizza when they think it's a snack? How do you sell a premium detergent to Hema, Rekha, Jaya and Sushma who are dancing to the tune of a low-priced one? What will make amma get into the habit of using a liquid hand-wash instead of just bar-soaping it up?

In general, we are tough with people we are buying things from. No *ji*, we don't roll over and wag our tails when the MNCs come out to play with us. (Or even the *lalas* for that matter.) They need to kindly adjust to our ways. So, from an international chain of iconic beef burgers comes the McAloo Tikki Burger, a uniquely Indian solution for the vegetarian Indian. And the world may be eating at that joint with all the fried chicken but what's *kukkad-shukkad* without a little *masala*? We will only settle for a fiery grilled or tandoori chicken equivalent, thank you very much.

A ham and cheese pizza may be a safe bet anywhere in the world; in India, though, the dish has had to reinvent itself into a *chicken tikka* pizza in the north and the no-onion, no-garlic Jain pizza in the west.

The vastness of the land, combined with the distinct identities of every region and their inherent sociocultural nuances, can be a nightmare to decipher. For the marketer, it can be about striking it lucky on the first try. Or it can take years of research and hits-and-misses. Or it may require consumer-centric product innovations that are strategically branded and smartly positioned. And, sometimes, it can take all of the above and more.

The cliché of the unique Indian exists for a reason.

Ones Upon a Time

AD-ING UP THE YEARS

Indians have always known a thing or two about advertising and marketing – especially where visual communication is concerned. The age-old paintings in the Bhimbetka caves as well as in Ajanta and Ellora are still telling people stories. Taking that tradition forward, we now use bright yellow or blue to paint entire Himalayan rock-faces to tell the world about the wonders of a certain washing powder or a cement brand. The towering genius of the medium is remarkable in itself.

Any child who has been on a road trip will tell you that houses on highways are great for huge wall-painted tyre ads. And the railway-train-ed kids learn that love can be found by calling the '*Rishtey-hi-rishtey*' number seen from trains chugging into railway stations.

Not so long ago, advertising often came across as entertainment – a literal break. It entered our subconscious and peopled our memories with wondrous characters and phrases.

It became a veritable *yaadon ki baaraat*.

So, that giant, buck-toothed rabbit that lives inside many of our heads is also forever singing, '*Karram-kurram, saat swaad mein* Lijjat Lijjat *papad.*' Some of us will also have Jalal Agha holding up a string of Pan Parag packets as the category-immortalizing jingle, 'Pan Parag, *pan masala!*' fills the background. Tell someone you are planning to give the boss the finger and you are likely to hear, 'What an idea, *sirji!*'

Love it or hate it, advertising is a part of popular culture, sometimes mimicking it and sometimes setting new trends. It is not always pretty or desirable but it is always evolving.

It all began, as they say, 'Once upon a time in Mumbai'. In 1905, an astute guy called B. Dattaram set up India's first advertising agency, Dattaram & Co. (which still exists). It was a milestone and reserved a place for him in Indian advertising history. At the time, the British were considered the gods of all that was luxurious and worthy of acquiring. They influenced opinion and fashion for the Indian upper crust. Naturally, they also influenced communication. So it's not surprising that India's oldest ads were not very Indian.

One of the ads created by Dattaram & Co. was for Westend Watches. Calling them, 'Always dependable,' the ad revolved around the very Western concept of Father Time, who featured in the ad as a hand-drawn figure complete with a scythe and a flowing beard.

However, it did not take long for marketing to evolve in the Indian context as well and for marketers to start catering to Indian audiences. By the 1930s, even local players were exploring unknown markets. In Kolkata, K.C. Das, whose father had invented the rosogulla, saw potential in vacuum-packing. He started canning the sweet which gave it a longer shelf life. Soon enough, it gained favour in other cities and, later, in other countries. Like him, many others realized that packaging, transportation and distribution could make a difference in the movement of products.

Back then, a lot of advertising was instinctive, especially outdoor advertising, which often consisted of wall paintings, painted shop shutters, signboards and sometimes live demonstrations. For example, Dalda hydrogenated oil was sold by sending people equipped with folding tables and kerosene stoves to villages to set up improvised food stalls. They got people to sample dishes which were cooked with Dalda to convince them that the taste was similar to that of ghee, while drilling in the fact that the price was less than half the cost of ghee.

When the British quit India, some of their legacies included products that straddled the two eras – Lipton's Tea, Afghan Snow beauty cream and Sunlight washing soap among them. Many of these brands had to rethink their advertising, though. Take Pears soap, for instance. It stayed with its advertising promise of purity, but it had to leave behind its habit of telling newly independent Indians that Pears soap was 'by appointment to the Emperor and Empress of India'. It also adopted the deified visuals seen in stylized Indian paintings.

As newer brands entered the market, Indian advertising continued to reflect the changing aspirations of the people. Socialist thinking gave rise to a new mood. In the 1950s, profit was not a much-liked word, patriotism counted for a lot and films like *Mother India* and *Naya Daur* gave expression to all that was considered good and worthwhile. You lent a hand in building a new India, you felt proud of having shaken off the rulers *and* of the tastes you had imbibed from them. The process of finding a uniquely Indian voice had begun.

When Lakmé was formed in 1952, it was named after the French opera, titled *Lakmé*, a French-ified pronunciation of the absolutely Indian 'Lakshmi' – the beauteous goddess of wealth. Filling the vacuum that was the Indian cosmetics space, it proved to be a masterstroke by Tata Oil Mills (Tomco). Among others, the film star Rekha too posed for it in her almost-famous days. 'Unmatched beauty,' the ad proclaimed, showcasing Lakmé Satin Glow Liquid Make-up and Ultra-silk Compact (which was 'sifted through pure silk', no less). Lakmé went on to become *the* name in beauty products. Generations of mothers and daughters adopted it, word of mouth affecting its sales as much as the advertising.

A couple of decades later, there were some brands that were definitely 'it' but not so many that you couldn't count them on two hands. Moti was *the* luxury soap, and where there was a Moti in the visual, could fat, glistening *motis* be left out? It was almost always shown in the company of, what else, strings of pearls.

Pond's Cold Cream, which had been around for a long, long time, promised to keep your skin rose-petal soft just as it had done for your mom.

When Lifebuoy re-launched in a big way in 1964, the song and dance was all around a sweaty, sporty guy lathering up to, '*Tandrusti ki raksha karta hai,* Lifebuoy. Lifebuoy *hai jahaan tandrusti hai wahaan!*'

Even if you tried, you could not avoid the 'Made for each other' couple in the ads for Wills (Navy Cut) cigarettes (with 'filter and tobacco perfectly matched'). They hung out from the 1960s right up to the new millenium.

In the years when Indira Gandhi's popularity was at its peak, so was her wardrobe of handloom saris. Handloom House was established in those days, inspired by Pupul Jayakar, the activist-revivalist of Indian handloom and handicrafts (and, therefore, of the omnipresent 'Indian culture'). Zeenat Aman was one of its early ad models. Sharmila Tagore, too, posed for saris in the early 1970s but it was to launch the 'new' technology in fabric – the 100 per cent polyester saris from Bombay Dyeing (yes, even polyester had its day).

By the 1980s, Rasna had become truly popular for its soft drink concentrates. Kids wanted to try every new flavour from 'khus' to 'rose' so they could swap tasting tales and indulge in one-upmanship. The innumerable glasses that emerged from each pack, as well as the convenience of making the drink, were enough to make most moms get on board.

In 1982, colour television began making inroads into our homes. Televisions changed what the average Indian saw of the world and how she saw it. From getting their music only via radio, people flitted to the new, magical world of options where music was accompanied by a video (okay, mostly of the *Chitrahaar* variety on Doordarshan) now available to them on TV.

Television started showing more assertive women. Rajani crusaded for her civic rights in the serial carrying her name, 'washing powder' Nirma frothed over in budget-conscious households, Lalitaji lauded her own *samajhdari* in making Surf the detergent of her choice.

A bold new look was in order for this emerging woman. Caught between 'being proud of Indian culture' while aspiring for Western affirmation, we collectively gaped at the glossy look of the Garden Vareli ads which smoothly wrapped up both worlds. Wearing a *pagdi*, Persis Khambatta – the actress rumoured to have OMG-shaved-her-head-for-a-Hollywood-movie (really?) – arrived on our televisions, draped unconventionally. Was it a sari? Was it an outfit? Was her turban an accessory or was it a glamorous cover-up of her hairless status? Enigmatic as it was, everyone was captivated with the ads, which signed off saying, 'You fascinate me.'

Far more conventional was the Chaplin-esque Cherry Charlie promoting Cherry Blossom shoe polish in the 1980s. For generations of well-schooled people for whom shiny shoes were non-negotiable (and who became that way because generations of teachers had pointed at their shoes and roared, '*Shoo paalish?*'), he was a fun motivator, obsessed with getting the perfect shine on his shoes but acquiring it in a lovable way.

This was also the time when, as a nation, we sang along with the Lok Seva Sanchar Parishad's '*Mile sur mera tumhaara*'. The national integration ad featuring Very Important Persons (VIPs) in sports, music and other walks of life sent pride coursing through the veins of every couch-patriot.

The early 1990s saw India embarking on its journey towards liberalization, though not without much hand-wringing and nervousness. When Sushmita Sen was crowned Miss Universe in 1994, the word Sen-sation rolled off newspaper presses and everyone's tongues. Instantly, Miss Universe became a brand here. Cosmetics companies were already eyeing the vast marketplace that was India and now the Indian woman was looking at them speculatively too.

Revlon was one of the first international cosmetics brands to arrive in the country, and as more and more international brands queued up, the Indian consumer was soon spoilt for choice. Just some decades earlier, we used to be a people for whom secure earnings and comfortable retirement were of prime concern. We liked our *sarkari* jobs, admired the 'simple' life and believed deeply in contentment.

Now, wanting more was no longer a sign of greed; it was simply a sign of the times. Not asking for more or not having aspirations was the new sin. As we kept up with our neighbours, metropolises as well as smaller communities began indulging in consumerism like never before.

Brands like Pepsi and Levi's, perceived to be the international 'cool', began making their presence felt. Meanwhile, you were also being urged by a young Salman Khan to sip Limca, which had 'isotonic salts to quench your thirst'. And if you were thinking of doing so on a train journey, you could just as well get yourself that old childhood favourite, Parle-G biscuits.

The joy felt by a family, a *mohalla* even, in possessing a scooter? It was aptly captured by '*Humara* Bajaj'. As for the joy of eating a Cadbury's Dairy Milk, it was celebrated with abandon (and running out on to a cricket pitch in a crowded stadium and rejoicing over the boyfriend's six with a joyous jig) in the '*Asli swaad zindagi ka*' ad.

Then the new millennium arrived, bringing with it even newer categories and ideas. Naukri.com had the right job for you if your boss's name was spelt 'H for Hitler, A for arrogant, R for rascal and I for idiot'.

There was Facebook.

There was also so much to Google.

Advertising had to take into account the Internet and a new infusion of terms – ad words, pay-per-click, SEOs and more. Banner ads no longer meant a message on a cloth strung across the street – it could also mean an ad on a website. Ad size was no longer just about half-page, full-page or also-ran-on-page; on the Internet, it could include 'weight'. And audiences were just called eyeballs.

Now, online social networks are the *tadka* of our lives. Without it, going for a holiday, eating at a restaurant or even good old exercising feels like boiled peeli daal. Allowing us to express ourselves and to communicate with each other are Instagram, Pinterest, Tumblr, Foursquare and so much more. People no longer just hail a cab, they tap on apps like Uber and Ola, telling cabbies exactly where to find them. If they walk, Pedometer takes care of calculating the steps (and the exercise). Indians are not lagging behind in anything, and are fast downloading apps, warming up to wearable devices and dabbling with augmented reality.

From the old hand-drawn print ads to the astoundingly well-produced television commercials of today from out-of-home experiential sessions to immersing people in the brand experience at their desktops, consumer engagement sure has come a long way.

Chaddi Pehan ke Fool Khila Hai

BAWDY, SHODDY HAPPENINGS

In romantic TV serials, when the boy shimmies up to 'the one', she glows incandescently and her hair whips around her face just like the storm being whipped up in her heart.

In romantic scenes in old Hindi movies, you know the young pair of lovers is doing 'it' when your screen is taken over by two beak-crossed *kabootar*s while the smug sound of their *guturr-goo* fills the air.

How else do you portray that kind of action?

It was the underwear ads that showed the way – along with some juice, deodorant, shoe and coffee ads. They depicted the aforementioned lovers in their *chaddi*s (and sometimes out of their *chaddi*s). Simple.

In underwear ads, a man in a *baniyan* can not only strut proudly in public spaces, he is an irresistible Chick Magnet when he does so.

The fully-clothed male need not worry, though – not as long as he is drinking 'juice'. Some ads have shown how beverages like juice and soda also make him that irresistible Chick Magnet we were talking about.

But for 100-per-cent-guaranteed irresistibility, a man has to spray copious amounts of deodorant. Sooner, rather than later, a woman (whatever her relationship status may be) will fling herself right onto his chest.

While some really head-turning ads have had these kind of themes, other ads have been noticeable because they indulged in 'loose talk' – of the sexist, classist or racist kind.

And while the aim of an ad may well be to simply attract attention, sometimes that attention turns out to be of absolutely the wrong kind – making people hem-and-'hawwww' instead of going, 'Wow!'

Amul Macho

If underwear ads are to be believed, the key to being Superman (that guy who's so proud of his *chaddi*, he wears it over his pants) is stepping out in branded undergarments, preferably the one your favourite Bollywood star claims to wear.

An underwear ad typically opens with a woman walking down a deserted street, late at night. A group of goons spots her. They make catcalls; she looks worried and starts walking faster. The men follow her. She starts running and so do they. She screams.

And suddenly...

Is it a bird?

Is it a plane?

No, it's *Chaddi-Baniyan* Man!

He is showing full body-*shoddy* as he is wearing only his undergarments. In his hurry to save the world, he has had no time to get decent.

You know the rest. This underdressed guy holds fully-dressed-for-party girl with one arm. With his other arm, he effortlessly flicks aside the bad guys. Meanwhile, his... err...assets are displayed, immodestly encased in a *laal/*

*peela/neela/*tiger-striped *chaddi.* Rising to the occasion is the music.

Most underwear ads for men were much the same.

Till Amul Macho decided to be different. Their ad starred a girl.

The story of the undergarments industry in India has been one of sensitivity, not in the ads, visuals and communication it has unleashed on consumers, but in the mindset of consumers. That is to say, Indian buyers have always been price sensitive. But over the years they have also become design and brand sensitive. Growing disposable income has brought with it a rising demand for branded, better-fitted and comfortable underwear. While this has helped in driving growth in the market as a whole, it has also forced innovation in design.

In the 1990s, more and more brands of men's underwear started becoming visible. Between 2000 and 2008, high-end *firang* brands entered the Indian market and underwear began turning into fashion. Who can forget the regrettable fad when men began wearing their jeans low enough to show off their underwear's elastic bands – sometimes showing off supposedly cool brand names and always showing off some really un-cool butt cracks.

Anyway, traditional white underwear is now just one part of a brave new world. Multiple options of colours, materials and styles are now available. For men, there are now tons of innerwear to consider – vests, sleeved vests, muscle vests, briefs, trunks, boxers, long underwear, etc.

The economy segment accounts for more than half the category while super-premium, premium and medium segments make up the rest.

Whoever said men think with their, *errm*, male part, did not have a clue about how much thought could go into clothing the said part.

But much thinking is exactly what some of the biggest players in the branded innerwear segment – VIP, Amul Macho, Rupa, Lux, Dixcy, among others – are doing.

For the manufacturers of Amul-branded innerwear, J.G. Hosiery Private Ltd, the projected turnover for 2007–08 was ₹210 crore.[1] Going forward, they were looking at investing on capacity and on brand building and therefore, advertising. When it comes to underwear brands, advertisements have always teamed up with male stars flaunting their wares. Salman Khan, Hrithik Roshan, Shah Rukh Khan, Saif Ali Khan, Sunny Deol – the list of underwear models is long and illustrious.

But what if there's no star? What if the perspective is not a man's but a woman's?

This is one of the things that makes the 2007 Amul Macho television commercial stand out. It showed only the woman. In fact, there is no man in the frame at all. He is represented solely by his *chaddis*, which the woman, something of a village belle, is shown washing at a pond.

[1] 'Amul Innerwear Plans Rs 80 Cr Expansion', *Economic Times*, 19 February 2008

Throughout the ad, she washes the man's underwear, her mouth contorting suggestively. As shocked villagers look on, one phrase is repeated rhythmically, excitedly reaching a peak, '*Yeh toh bada toingg hai! Yeh toh bada toingg hai! Yeh toh bada toingg hai! Yeh toh bada toingg hai!*' The ad ends with the woman stretching the underwear in her hands, while the voice-over concludes, 'Amul Macho. Crafted for fantasies.'

It is evident that *chaddi ke peechhey* story *hai.* Scrubbing his laundry makes her relive the night she and the man have spent together. Yes, the underwear is making her lust for his under-ware.

'*Yeh toh bada toingg hai!*' as an expression was intended to communicate the overwhelmingly pleasurable nature of these fantasies.

But underwhelmed consumers shouted back, '*Yeh toh bada* vulgar *hai!*'

Protests were lodged and cases were filed. While the Advertising Standards Council of India had cleared it for public viewing, the Ministry of Information and Broadcasting censored the ad on the grounds that it was indecent, vulgar and suggestive. Even today, the '*Yeh to bada toingg hai*' ad is considered by some to be one of the most sexually explicit ads in the history of Indian advertising.

Meanwhile, Amul Macho continues to be a strong brand in Bihar, Uttar Pradesh and Jharkhand, with a significant presence in Andhra Pradesh and Tamil Nadu as well.

In the under-dressed pantheon of male film stars showing their *chaddis* to the world, the female showstopper, Sana Khan, will long be remembered for her association with the Amul Macho men's underwear.

(Though the orangutan in a later Amul Macho ad was pretty hard to ignore too.)

Calida

If men's underwear ads seem to like courting controversy, women's lingerie ads do not fight shy either. Why should they when there's a lingerie market – worth around ₹11,000 crore in 2015[2] – to get intimate with?

Desi brands such as Soie, Pretty Secrets, Calibra, Clovia and Sonari fight it out in a market that is no longer black and white. It's not even skin-coloured. Bright primary colours fill in bra charts. Rumour has it that some women even like wearing Batman next to their skin and Warner Bros. along with Ginza Industries' Soie helps them do just that.

But before lingerie shopping became fraught with choices and much before superheroes started frequenting bra designs, there was an incident in 1998 involving the Swiss. At the time, the Indian undergarments industry had been seeing a surge in activity. The men's market was already flooded with advertisements which had superstars brandishing their underwear. Older women

[2] Ganguly, Sharmana, 'Lingerie Market Gets a Makeover as Indian Women Experiment with Colours, Designs and Cuts', *Economic Times*, 6 July 2015

had dim memories of Maidenform, Jockey and Jantzen entering their lives in the 1960s and exiting not too long after. When you went shopping, you came across existing brands like Libertina, and if you went through a few magazine ads, you knew VIP had Feelings.

In 1995, Page Industries Ltd launched Jockey in India for the second time and, in 1996, Lovable World Trading Company's product line was also launched in the country. From then on, international brands streamed in. One of them was the Swiss brand, Calida.

Calida was from Natural Textiles Ltd, which came to India as an equal joint venture with the Phulchand Group, a Mumbai-based textiles and commodities exporter. A leader in the Swiss market, Calida was also a top drawer in Germany and France.

What was unique about Calida was that it was one of the first brands in India to retail both men's underwear and women's lingerie under one name. Competition was everywhere. Among upmarket labels for men and women, there were Vanity Fair, Lovable and Liberblu, Jockey and Rivolta. So it became important to first build brand awareness.

The idea was to highlight that the undergarments were Swiss and build on that brand association in a playful way. But in a market that is about displaying underwear, getting provocative is just an ad approval away.

Calida's 1998 ad featured Dino Morea, a popular ramp model at the time, along with the one-who-was-yet-to-be a Bollywood star, Bipasha Basu. For most of us, the only Swiss experience was the sensuous one of sinking our teeth into Swiss chocolate. Apparently, Dino Morea was reminded of the same thing. Only, he was sinking his teeth into underwear – Bipasha Basu's panties, to be exact. Along with that indelible image of him pulling off Bipasha's inedible panties with his teeth was the message, 'And you thought your appetite for indulgence could only be whetted by Swiss chocolates.'

In hindsight, the copy may have been tongue-in-cheek but it wasn't too clever. People missed both the tongue and the cheek and bared their fangs instead. They did not approve of the visualization the communication conjured up, and eventually, the ad was banned. Later, Bipasha Basu claimed she had not even known the visuals were being put in ads. She said the photographs were shot privately and were not meant to be used.

Today, the Calida ad is all but forgotten. So while no one gets their panties into a twist over it, it does come up whenever ad notoriety is being discussed.

Zatak

What does a man need to seduce a woman?

Charm?

Intelligence?

A sense of humour?

No, all he needs is the right deodorant. Or so our deodorant ads tell us.

In 2009, the market for fragrances was pegged at about ₹470 crore[3] and was characterized by low consumption. The conundrum facing manufacturers was how to turn deodorant usage into a widespread habit.

Sex has been the traditional benefit offered to the male consumer. Therefore, it seemed obvious that sex (or the thought of it) in a traditional setting would make a brand easier to identify with. Sure, it just might raise some eyebrows but that was a side-effect that couldn't be helped. After all, the idea of sexual collisions in deodorant ads was a tried-and-tested one.

Axe, from Hindustan Unilever Ltd, had used this scenario quite successfully in its global communication, which centred on women going wild when they came across men who had used the deodorant. (Some years ago, an Axe Dark Temptation television commercial even strayed into cannibalism. It showed women taking bites out of an irresistible chocolate man who had used the chocolate-scented Axe deo. He ended up getting bitten in the bottom and losing a limb.)

While Axe was the biggie in a market that was promising and full of potential, there were other brands looking for action, among which were Fa Men Xtreme from Henkel India Ltd, Denver deodorant from Vanesa Care Pvt. Ltd and Wild Stone from McNroe Chemical Pvt. Ltd.

---

[3] Mehra, Priyanka, 'Sexual Overtones Land Two Deodorant Ads Under ASCI Scanner', *Livemint*, 21 July 2009

To Wild Stone goes the distinction of taking the seduction story into almost-Bhabhi territory. In 2007, it released a television commercial set in a Durga puja celebration. So far, so ordinary. Then you saw your neighbourhood Bengali *boudi* (bhabhi) bumping into a man – not your average Bengali *bhadralok* but one who has smartly drenched himself with copious amounts of Wild Stone deodorant.

Aah, this proves to be her undoing (literally). It becomes obvious that the smell is such a turn-on that it makes for a fantasy that just needs to be played out. 'Wild by nature' you are told about Wild Stone (and its users) in the end.

Was the ad censored? Yes. But the full version continues to play on YouTube to the collective delight of lakhs of viewers.

For deodorant marketers, this seemed to be a viable strategy. The truth agreed on by most communication in the category was that good fragrance could make a bad boy out of just about anybody. Just one whiff from his armpit was enough to overpower a(ny) woman's senses. There really was no reason to think out of the box. Having said that, even with this limited a platform, some brands showed how you could create waves.

You know how some names give you a sense of things to come? Well, it certainly is true for the slick-sounding Zatak which came from the house of Paras Pharmaceuticals for the smelling pleasure of the ladies.

In 1999, Zatak released an ad film which showed a man losing a button and his bhabhi losing control. As she tried to stitch the button on to the shirt her brother-in-law was wearing, his deodorant made her 'do things'. 'Just Zatak her,' the ad helpfully told you in the end.

Then, in 2010, another television commercial opened on a setting that had become a cliché (or is it classic?) thanks to Bollywood. A newly married woman is artistically arranged on a bed, expecting her newly-minted husband to come into the bedroom and get the *suhaag-raat* on its way. But suddenly she gets a whiff of something – something good. On going to the window she sees a neighbour eyeing her. Obviously he is up to no good because he has that thing that creates magic, that good-smelling thing, *that* deodorant. It is obviously a bride-lure to boot, because you then see her taking off her wedding ring. The ad ends with the message (say it with appropriate *ssszzz* sounds): 'Just Zatak her'.

Slick, huh?

Probably a little too slick for the Ministry of Information and Broadcasting. It asked the Advertising Standards Council of India to look into the ad for obscenity and sexual explicitness. In spite of the controversy, or perhaps because of it, the suggestive positioning of Paras Pharmaceuticals' Zatak has high recall. And so, many years later, you can still find the 'Uncensored full version of the naughty Zatak Deo TVC about a newly wed' online, tickling the fancies of over three lakh viewers.

Another 2011 Zatak ad shows a young man visiting a dentist who happens to be female. What he suffers from is unclear because, to cloud issues for the viewer, he has sprayed himself with Zatak Deo. This results in the dentist shutting her eyes and moaning suggestively. When our male lead tells her he has a toothache, she starts removing (what else?) his shirt. Hippocrates-hypocrites be damned, soon her white coat is no longer on her even as her buttons pop open to reveal some cleavage. Yes, that's how you 'just Zatak her', the ad seems to say.

A Zatak Cool Talc commercial, also released in 2011, shows all the action taking place in a *darzi ki dukaan*. The old tailor master's son is measuring up a sari-blouse clad lady. As the tape measure goes over various parts of her body, she feels the coolness of an ice-cube sliding down. Because of the fragrance in the talc he has just used, she cannot keep her hands off him. The brand succinctly tells you, '*thandaa, thandaa,* cool, cool. Just Zatak her.' (Shame on all you frigid prickly heat powder brands. Never thought of extending your product benefits to help those who were not part of the *ghamori*-afflicted scratching masses did you?)

That was the year India's Ministry of Information and Broadcasting stepped in on some ad films with storylines like those above. It asked brands like Wild Stone, Addiction Deo, Set Wet Zatak, Denver Deo and Axe to either change their television commercials or stop airing them, because advertisements portraying women 'lustily hankering after men under the influence of such deodorants' offended 'good taste and decency' by 'tickling libidinous male instincts'.

AC Black Apple Juice

There is a Japanese cartoon on television, the dubbed Hindi version of which is very popular with kids all over the country. It has a little boy-hero whose father is sometimes seen stumbling home – happy, his nose red, voice slurry and eyes boozy. If asked why, even your six-year-old will explain to you, very kindly, that *uske* father *ne aaj thoda zyaada* juice *pee liya.*

There you have it. You *can* have a good time even with juice. Especially when mentioning the word 'alcohol' is prohibited.

In the cartoon, it's not entirely clear whether it's the dubbing guys who cleaned up the reference to alcohol or whether it was originally written that way. Like those television commercials – the ones which show men and women dancing with abandon because they are high – high on Bagpiper Soda, of course. Or under the influence of Bacardi CDs. Or having a super time because they are playing *teen patti* with Officer's Choice playing cards.

So how did we as a nation learn to be so drunk with happiness over such mundane things?

As liquor markets go, India ranks among the top three in the world. In 2016, the consumption of alcohol in India was estimated to be ₹1.46 trillion.[4]

We get *talli* on whisky, rum, brandy, vodka, gin, beer and wine. Of these, while wine shows a high rate of growth in demand, whisky wins hands down in popularity.

While some people may think it is up to the dads in cartoons whether or not to drink juice – *merey baap ka kya jaata hai* and all that – our nation's founding fathers may disagree. Even our Constitution disagrees.

The Constitution of India encourages prohibition. As the Directive Principles of State Policy (Article 47 of the Constitution) say, 'The State shall endeavour to bring about prohibition of the consumption, except for medicinal purpose, of intoxicating drinks and of drugs which are injurious to health.'

While governments want to do just enough to show disapproval of high-spiritedness, they do not want to let go of the significant tax revenue they collect from the manufacture and sale of these intoxicants.

This brings us to the much-debated subject of advertising for alcohol. Advertising helps in establishing a brand with consumers and makes them think of it every time they visit the nearest *theka*. So while prohibition may not be completely possible (revenue wise), what

---

[4] Kashyap, Karan, 'How Startups are Catering to India's $35B Liqouor Market, The 3rd Largest in the World', *Forbes*, 27 March 2017

is possible is cutting off communication between the manufacturer and the consumer. (This discovery is the point where someone in charge of the rule book must have said *Eureka!*)

This decision was followed by the usual debates over 'but advertising is not the bad boy' and 'isn't industry self-regulation the answer to problems?' Nevertheless, the Cable Television Networks (Regulation) Act 1995, after the Cable Television Networks Rules 1994, came into force. This banned all direct advertising pertaining to liquor, tobacco and cigarettes.

Every liquor, tobacco and other *nasheela padarth* manufacturer took note of the word 'direct'. They went underground and fathered innocuous products (like soda) which could carry the brand name in advertisements while showing 'happy' people – really 'happy' people.

Surrogate advertising had arrived.

For a game with sketchy rules, the players in surrogate advertising are many.

One of the first brands to adopt surrogate advertising was Bagpiper, which came up with ads for Bagpiper soda. Basically, the marketing hope was that when you saw an ad for Bagpiper soda, you would say, 'Mmm, feel like pouring myself a Bagpiper whisky.'

McDowell's No.1, Officer's Choice, Haywards, Royal Challenge, White Mischief, Antiquity and Romanov followed suit. Royal Stag decided to use Bollywood and cricketing stars. But it was Kingfisher, till then mostly associated with its beer, that gave its surrogate advertising a scale that would be hard to miss. Soon bottled water, soda, calendars and fashion shows were all carrying the Kingfisher brand name. (As we all know, when Mallya shops, he doesn't stop.) United Breweries had promoted Kingfisher Soda by using sports imagery for its first few ads. Soon, a mix of music, sports and Caribbean themes personified the brand.

When Bacardi came in, it had similar imagery in its ads which signed off with Bacardi Blast music CDs.

The tobacco industry came up with the Red & White Bravery Awards, Four Square White Water Rafting, Godfrey Phillips Bravery Awards and Wills Lifestyle Clothing Line.

Not to be left behind, the *gutkha* industry borrowed some glamour with Manikchand sponsoring the Filmfare Awards.

So you had a cigarette manufacturer launching and advertising its fashion label; you had a well-known whisky brand making television commercials for club soda; and you had absolutely jaw-dropping, parental-guidance-required-ads where grown men and women did very grown-up things after downing a shot of apple juice.

Yes, we're talking about AC Black Apple Juice.

Jagatjit Industries owned the brand AC Black Whisky. In 2002–03, when the cricket World Cup came up, it guaranteed a mega-audience of television viewers. What better opportunity to advertise?

The film opens in a bar. A drink is being poured from a bottle which prominently shows the label AC Black Apple Juice. A man picks up the glass to drink just as a woman in a little black dress walks into the bar and sits a short distance away.

What follows is a story of plunging drink levels leading to a plunging neckline. Each time he sips his drink, the neckline of her dress drops – from showing collar-bone right up to (or down to) showing cleavage. All interspersed with the guy's eyes widening and smile broadening and – in case you missed the connection – his looking at her through his whisky glass. His AC Black Apple Juice glass, that is.

Lest you think the brand was indulging in lewd-ity of only the male kind, he suddenly looks down and realizes his buttons are open and he is showing his... chest (what did you think?). Just then the woman he's been watching raises her glass of AC Black Apple Juice (you would never have guessed) in acknowledgment of his mental undressing and smiles. Because, hey, she's been mentally undressing him too.

The ad signs off by telling you, '*Kuch bhi ho sakta hai!*'

Anticipating a rise in demand because of this noteworthy commercial, the company rolled out whisky (not apple juice) worth crores into stores. This was despite it traditionally being a lean season for sales. Pumping money into advertising, it booked airtime for the entire period of the World Cup.

Alas, whether or not the commercial worked was something they never found out. There were protests about the ad and it was summarily yanked off the air. The shocked company mulled over going to court, but finally decided against it. Today, the ad continues to live on in memories. And, of course, on YouTube.

This brings home the ubiquity of surrogate advertising today. Companies tiptoe around the law and sometimes even just use social media messaging to promote products that build brand recall. There is also controversy around alcohol companies using socially responsible platforms (like 'Don't drink and drive') as a form of surrogate advertising.

The questions remain many. If a product is considered bad for people by the government, should its advertising be banned? Or its sales?

Or should certain products simply be considered beyond human interference – after all, could there a divine, mystical reason that beer sounds so much like cheer?

Slice

Someone once said, 'A little coitus never hoitus.' Or, as a passage from an ancient Indian text says, '*The horse and mare, the bull and deer, form the high union, while the horse and deer form the highest union. On the female side, the elephant and bull, the mare and hare, form low unions, while...*'

Apparently, the animals represent people who are trying to have a union, that is, sex. This passage shows how the ancient Indians knew a thing or two about the birds and the bees and the hares and the mares. We had passion or *kaam*. And we had the *Kama Sutra*.

Apparently now, Indians have *aam*. And we have the Aamsutra.

Or so Slice tells us.

To the Indian, a mango is no *aam* thing. When it's in season, we see mangoes everywhere.

For example, when a Bollywood male-star-wannabe does the classic take-off-the-damn-shirt act, our netizens look at the man-boobs he has revealed and comment, 'Those totally look like *Dussehri aam*.'

People float political parties with *aam* people in it.

Cool desis even call us mango people in a banana republic.

Mango is serious business, made all the more serious because the mango season is short-lived. So having year-round mango drinks competing for our tastebuds is completely logical. What is unique is the way they compete for our attention.

In 2016, the total value of the mango-drinks market was around ₹6,300 in India.[5] From 1976 onwards, a sizeable share of the fruit drinks market has belonged

---

[5] Malviya, Sagar, 'Parle Agro's Frooti Beats PepsiCo's Slice to Win Back No. 2 Slot After a Decade', *Economic Times*, 12 May 2016

to Maaza, which was owned by Parle and is now owned by Coca-Cola. Most players in the market have always tried to equate their mango drink to the fruit itself – as in, 'Mango Frooti, fresh and juicy' or '*Laalach* for *aam*, Maaza *hai naam!*'

When PepsiCo launched Slice in 1993, the brand needed to make its presence felt. It tried by being the 'Real mango flavor' and 'A provider of simple joy'. Somehow, taglines like 'Simple joy *ka ras*' just did not catch on.

Then in 2008, Slice was relaunched with a new formulation and taste, a brand-new look with new graphics and packaging *and* a brand-new communication idea. The intent was to own the platform of pleasure of the *aam* kind.

All competing brands were talking about the deliciousness of mango and its flavour, which is what is special about the fruit. But what if you could highlight the *pleasure* of eating a mango? Mango-eating has always been the stuff slurpy, sloppy moments are made of. The task for Slice was to take the slurpiness and sloppiness into the realm of fantasy and build on the sensuality and indulgence of the experience.

It helped that the brand ambassadress decided on was someone the entire nation was Googling, YouTubing and generally heart-throbbing over: Katrina Kaif.

That year, to the land of Khajuraho, Slice gifted Aamsutra. Yes, the K was missing. And yes, that was the idea. Punny but true.

Aamsutra stayed true to its core idea over the years. Shot in classic seduction style, the commercials featured Katrina Kaif demonstrating the principles of 'Aamsutra' or the art of experiencing pure mango pleasure with the all-new Slice.

One television commercial shows Katrina with her hair blowing back sensuously as she arranges flowers and candles. There is an air of anticipation as she slowly settles down. Soon enough, it becomes evident that she is actually getting ready for the business of pleasuring herself – by drinking from a bottle of Slice. When she does, the shots are all about her indulging herself with the drink.

And then her boyfriend walks in, obviously thinking Katrina has been waiting for him. D-uh, little does he know... But, of course, he is incidental to the experience of Slice Aamsutra. Pure Mango Pleasure.

The ad was educative, to say the least. So *that* is how you eat a mango? Slowly and sensuously, while wiping off the juices? Like Katrina Kaif in the ad? Why on earth didn't our parents teach us to languorously savour the fruit instead of letting us go greedily for the *guthlee*?

Over the years, Katrina's love for Slice has taken on legendary proportions and has remained constant in an ever-changing world.

✓ Holi-playing Katrina – check.

✓ Playful Katrina – check.

✓ Bespectacled corporate Katrina – check.

The communication pushed on with the theme – putting Katrina in a rainforest; Katrina in a bottle, underwater, breathlessly waiting to be rescued; Katrina eagerly waiting to meet fans who will find 'her' number under Slice bottle crowns.

Whether you agree with the idea of mixing mangoes with pleasure or not, there is no denying that the communication is seductively head-turning and clutter breaking, with fantasy being the primary theme.

As of March 2016, Tropicana Slice had 23.4 per cent share of India's ₹6,300 crore mango-drinks category. Frooti's share was 25.6 per cent while Maaza from Coca-Cola was at the top with a 48 per cent share.[6]

Tiptoeing the line between sexual and sensual, the aim for Slice is still what it has always been – licking the competition.

Move over *aam aadmi*. As Katrina demonstrated, you don't stand a chance against the *aam aurat*.

Nando's

Vasco da Gama
Went to Panama
Took off his pajama

---

[6] Malviya, Sagar, 'Parle Agro's Frooti Beats PepsiCo's Slice to Win Back No. 2 Slot After a Decade', *Economic Times*, 12 May 2016

And showed his...(err, it is that fruit that begins with a *ban* and ends with an *ana.)*

Shy away from saying it all you want, but little children can scream out the whole chant, even though it refers to the famous Portuguese explorer in a decidedly non-childlike way. And, childishly, some big brands can scream out such things too.

Vasco da Gama may or may not have had exhibitionist tendencies but he was definitely the guy responsible for the discovery of new lands and (therefore) new spices and new recipes.

The same cannot be said of his culinary modern-day counterpart, Nando's. While it definitely is one of the biggest success stories of round-the-world foodie integration with its claim of 'Portuguese chicken meets African inspiration meets India', Nando's may, on one occasion, just have been caught with its pants down.

In the new world, contrary to what some off-colour rhymes might suggest, it was not just the banana that was making its way around but also the otherwise flightless chicken.

When Nando's wanted to advertise its Afro-Portuguese inspired, flame-grilled peri-peri chicken, naughty may have been exactly what it had in mind. But the spice levels on their menu can never compete with the heat their newspaper ad generated.

But first, some background to their story.

Nando's started in 1987 in South Africa. Its star offering has always been its flame-grilled peri-peri chicken. Over the years, Nando's has become a global chain, with over 1,300 restaurants in 27 countries. South Africa, Australia, the US, the UK and India have the special distinction of being markets that have company-owned and company-run restaurants.

Just like it did for Vasco da Gama so many centuries ago, for Nando's too, India promised to be a land with a distinct affinity for spice. Additionally, Indians are enthusiastically discovering dishes from around the world, and have both the money and the willingness to spend on unlocking these culinary experiences.

And so Nando's arrived in India in 2010.

In 2015, India as a fast-food market was estimated (by the market research firm Euromonitor) to be worth a gargantuan ₹1,01,770 crore. And Nando's was all set to cluck its way across the land. The not-to-be-missed-out-on Portuguese *kukkad* was their world-conquering signature dish – peri-peri chicken. The chicken is marinated for 24 hours and then served with the level of heat that the customer chooses. The sauces vary from lemon and herb to mild, hot and extra hot.

Things were heating up just nicely when suddenly Nando's found itself in a hot mess.

The brief must have been ordinary enough – to create an inviting ad on the delicious attributes of Nando's chicken. But, there's something about the word 'chicken' that seems to lend itself to descriptions you never hear in the context of the word *kukkad*. Adjectives like 'hot', 'legs' and 'fiery' seem to encourage advertising copywriters and marketers to get carried away.

The ad appeared in one of the nation's favoured daily newspapers. It was an open invitation to readers: 'Try something you can grab with both hands,' invited the headline. To leave no doubt whatsoever, the copy went on to explain, 'We don't mind if you touch our buns or breasts or even our thighs. Whatever you're into, enjoying a Nando's meal with your hands is always recommended.' A second ad had a headline that said, 'Try something that shows off a bit of skin.'

They were talking about chicken. Everyone got that. And yet they didn't. Was Nando's telling folks that its meat was like a woman? Or that a woman is meat?

Highly 'sexist', most outraged people said.

The language used in the ads caused quite a twitter. Jammu and Kashmir politician Omar Abdullah tweeted about it, asking Nando's if their food was so inedible that they had to rely on lines from a C-grade movie to sell it.

The clucking on social media continued with users slamming the chain. Tasteless, in particular, was one invective that must have hurt. They were also told that their communication was vulgar, offensive and it reinforced objectification of women.

There was much 'filing of complaint' and 'signing of petition'. At the very least, an apology was called for and when it came, it was seemingly heartfelt. Nando's India stated, 'We sincerely apologize for any offence caused by our ad published today. Our intent was not to offend anyone. We promise to do better.'[7]

In the long run, the 'chick' talk may not have had much effect on sales and, as with all things, Nando's seems to have been forgiven. But as an incident, this is one that is unlikely to be forgotten.

Kalyan Jewellers

We may say *sona-chandi* in the same breath but our daughters will always be named Sona. Have you ever met a Chandi?

India's love affair with gold is a cliché but we can't seem to snap out of it. In 2011, India reportedly imported more gold than any other country, around one-fifth of the global supply that year, which is equivalent to nearly all the gold the Swiss have stashed away in their central bank vaults.[8]

Jewellery has always been about status and security, should you (touch wood) fall on bad times. We have all grown up on stories from the Partition when people residing on the Pakistan side of the Radcliffe line stitched ornaments into the hems of their petticoats and left their

[7] Agnihotri, Sanjana, 'Sexist or not: Nando's Latest Print Ad is Raising Hell on Social Media', *India Today*, 29 March 2016

[8] 'Why do Indians Love Gold?', *Business Insider*, 23 November 2013

homes to come to Hindustan. Or dug a hole in their backyard and buried a stash, hoping to retrieve it later. (Imagine the number of residents of Lahore and Karachi with kitchen gardens that could regurgitate jewels instead of *gobhi*. If only they knew.)

But if there's one state in India that is known for its gold, it is Kerala. Everyone knows of Kerala's '*lau*' for gold. Malayali '*Gelf*' returnees grabbing their electronic items from the airport luggage belts are themselves human conveyor belts for the gold chains they are bringing home.

In the 1990s, while pan-Indian brands like Tanishq and Gitanjali Gems were making their presence felt, Kalyanaraman's in Thrissur was an established textile business that specialized in wedding finery. Customers began urging the store to also provide jewellery so it could be a one-stop wedding shop, and by 1994, that is what the business set out to do. At the time, Kerala already had a few established jewellery stores – Malabar Gold, Chemmanur, Josco and Alukkas, to name a few.

Despite all the local and national competition, Kalyanaraman's jewellery store did really well. As it expanded, it began relying on brand ambassadors to advertise its jewellery. Since timelessness and inter-generational appeal was key, the brand ambassadors were either regional film stars or people related to the stars. So while Shivaraj Kumar was chosen for his own star status in Karnataka, he is also Kannada superstar Rajkumar's son. Tamil star Prabhu Ganesan is the son of the legendary Sivaji Ganesan. Telugu star Nagarjuna Akkineni as well as Malayalam star Manju Warrier are also associated with Kalyan Jewellers because of their regional star power. Amitabh Bachchan and Aishwarya Rai Bachchan, on the other hand, are the brand's ambassadors at a pan-India level.

Kalyan Jewellers became one of the pioneers in standardizing jewellery buying and offering certifications. Recognizing the fact that the country was made up of different markets, it made an effort to cater to regional tastes. But even while keeping local preferences in mind, it took its signature designs across the country.

So it seemed a perfectly logical move when, in 2015, Kalyan Jewellers decided to release an advertisement that was not just local in flavour but was also in keeping with its persona of being a national player. The idea was to present royalty, timeless beauty and elegance. Who better than Aishwarya Rai Bachchan, former Miss World, and their very own brand ambassadress, to showcase their products?

The advertisement featured the actress reclining comfortably on a chaise longue. Behind her was a painting of a thin, dark-skinned child holding a giant parasol over her, protecting her from the shining sun. (No matter that she could outshine the sun itself with the ornate jewellery she was wearing.)

The reference was clear, if a little thoughtless. It seemed to be an attempt to recreate paintings from a couple of centuries ago when European (read white) noblewomen sat around while 'native' (read dark) servants did all the work. And it was quite the norm for many of the servants to be underage.

On seeing the ad in the morning newspaper, the reactions were instantaneous. First of all, people did a quick check to see whether they had time-travelled and woken up a few centuries ago. Then they sat down to tweet, post protests on Facebook and register their dismay in print. The ad and its models brought to the fore accusations of racism, classism and ageism.

In an open letter to Aishwarya Rai Bachchan, a group of activists – which included a former chairperson of the National Commission for Protection of Child Rights – told her that the ad was 'insidiously racist' and that she herself seemed to represent 'aristocracy from a bygone era – bejewelled, poised and relaxing while an obviously underage slave-child, very dark and emaciated, struggles to hold an oversized umbrella over your head.'

The letter went on to say, 'As an influential member of the Indian film industry and a popular star with a large fan following, we trust that you wish to use your image in a manner that promotes progressive thought and action, and would not knowingly promote regressive images that are racist and go against child rights.'

That is to say, the very 'fair' lady as opposed to the 'dark' child was a deliberate visual effect. The ad was not just racist, it also showed serfdom and child labour to be acceptable.

The company apologized for inadvertently causing offence and Aishwarya Rai Bachchan's publicist replied that the actress had no clue about the final ad because she was photographed against a plain background.

Well, what can be photoshopped-in can also be photoshopped-out. And that is exactly what happened. The ad was withdrawn and then re-released without the image of the slave-child.

The controversy did not seem to affect business, though. Apparently, very few people would stop buying from a brand because it displayed its ignorance and social ills in an advertisement. The 'open letter' making the rounds on Twitter did not upset the target audience. The letter itself was noticed mostly because it was addressed to Aishwarya Rai Bachchan.

In 2015, Kalyan Jewellers had similar revenue and margins as Tanishq, and in January 2016, the company announced that it would hit the 100-showroom mark by the end of the financial year by adding 14 new showrooms.[9]

Which tells us that for us, as far as buying jewellery is concerned, we don't have much room for negativity. But we always have room for more.

[9] Ghosal, Sutanuka, 'Kalyan Jewellers Will Hit the 100 Showroom Mark by FY16 End', *Economic Times*, 27 January 2016

Ford Figo

It may be called a boot or a trunk in other countries but in India the posterior region of a car is always called the dicky. It is one of our inheritances from the British.

The dicky is that black hole that throws back spanners, spare tyres and sometimes a pack of chips at us. It's where the guards at the mall poke around looking for the bombs we might have stowed away. And, in 2013, in a particularly unfortunate incident, it's where an enthusiastic bunch of people decided to place some ladies.

Bound and gagged, to boot.

India saw approximately 2.03 million sales of passenger cars in 2011–12.[10]

It was a large pie and understandably everyone wanted a share as evidenced by the significant number of car ads visible.

Advertising often reflects the aspirations of the target audience and tries to tap into their interests. What advertisers showcase depends on the segment being addressed. Sometimes, though, advertising can simply showcase short-sightedness.

Maybe that is how, in 2013, there came an unreleased but absolutely unforgettable series of ads created with

[10] Raj, Amit, 'Passanger Car Sales Fall for First Time in 12 Years', *Livemint*, 10 April 2013

Ford Figo in mind, showcasing a feature that may be of interest to the buyer – its extra-large dicky/boot/trunk.

The three communication pieces featured caricatured illustrations. The theme running through the ads was that of a famous person driving away in a Ford Figo, the boot of which accommodated three people connected with the person in focus in some way. Yup, that's how big the boot was. Oh, and the people in the trunk had been bound and gagged by the driver. It was a kidnapping of sorts.

The thought was completed by the line: 'Leave your worries behind' (in the Figo's extra-large boot).

One ad had a Schumacher lookalike driving the Figo with Sebastian Vettel, Lewis Hamilton and Fernando Alonso lookalikes imprisoned in his car's boot.

Things started unravelling with the ad that featured a caricature of the former Italian prime minister, Silvio Berlusconi (of the alleged bunga bunga parties and 17-year-old prostitute infamy) flashing a peace sign, driving away with three scantily clad women, bound and gagged in the trunk of his Ford Figo.

Then came the ad that showed Paris Hilton's double winking as she drove away with a caricatured Kim Kardarshian and two other girls trapped in her car's boot. Bound and gagged, of course.

And then the boot kicked back.

The ads were uploaded on a popular website that showcased advertising work (not always released) from across the world and attracted comments, compliments as well as vitriolic name-calling on a daily basis. It was a place advertising folks could parade their creative skills.

As the controversy started raging, the posters went viral and were shared across countries and markets. The reach was far more than the creators could have dreamed of. The ads became some of the most viewed pieces of ad creatives ever.

But whether at all Paris Hilton or Silvio Berlusconi were great ideas as mascots and sales drivers is a debate that ended before it could begin. Outraged people talked of the irresponsibility, indecency and immorality of portraying entrapped women, of equating them with baggage and of treating the matter as a joke in the public space. That, too, in a country that was raging with protests and demands of sensitivity after the Nirbhaya case, one of the most horrific rape cases to have ever been reported in India.

Ford felt the anger internationally. The company stated that they were as shocked as anyone else because the ads had never come up for approval and that there was no way that they would have been approved.

The advertising agency said the posters had never gone into paid media; the site's administrator took the ads down; the agency apologized to Ford in particular and the world in general; and many heads rolled before there was some kind of closure.

Last but not the least, Daniela Santanchè, formerly an undersecretary in Berlusconi's government, told the *Telegraph*, 'Depicting women as prisoners in the car is stupid. Mr Berlusconi treats women as princesses, not prisoners.'

Not a pleasant tale and one with a moral to boot – always check the dicky for objects of a debatable nature.

Tuff

The year was 1995. At the time, people liked to use sneakers as accessories. They hung out in them, they lounged in them and they partied in them. Oh, and some people actually used them for sports.

Scenting an opportunity in a nascent market, Phoenix, a company already manufacturing shoes for foreign labels, decided to promote its own brand, Tuff.

The result was a jaw-dropping ad that first released in two magazines, *Cine Blitz* and G. But it was not until the ad-image appeared in a news item for *Sunday Mid-Day*, that the controversy started.

In the image, two of India's foremost models, Milind Soman and Madhu Sapre, stood torso to torso, stark naked, looking boldly into the camera, while an extremely embarrassed python hung shyly around their body parts. Oh, and there was one more minor detail. The models were wearing Tuff shoes.

The copy, too, was minimalistic.

'Hiss. And hers. Tuff. Hardwear for feet.'

The rest is hisstory. Until then an unknown brand, Tuff, became a household name for a while with the ad immortalizing Tuff's brand recall. Though, unfortunately, recall did not mean much as far as sales were concerned.

As for the man, woman and serpent scenario? It definitely did not turn out to be the Garden of Eden if the cases piling up were any indication. The social service branch of Mumbai Police registered a case of vulgarity against the supermodels, while the Wildlife Protection Act was invoked against the advertising agency for the allegedly illegal use of the python and for animal cruelty.

Today, the brand is not notorious (or even seeking notoriety) anymore. It took 14 years for the courts to finally acquit the supermodels, with a court ruling even saying that it was important to take into account the artistic and literary value of the material.

In Indian advertising folklore, Madhu, Milind (and the python) remain entwined happily ever after.

As they say, Tuff times do not last but Tuff people do.

KamaSutra

Sex seemed to actually be *yawn-sambandh* in the year 1991. The land of Khajuraho and the *Kama Sutra* was suffering from acute sexual shyness. More often than not, condom advertisements were sleep-inducing or depicted the products as family-planning tools. Then came a brand campaign that was anything but yawn-worthy.

When the J.K. Ansell Group decided to launch a brand of condoms, they took pleasure and sensuality, not safety, as the platform. They also decided on the name

'KamaSutra', which was different from what was usual in the category.

The launch ad created a sensation. It displayed the undeniably hot Pooja Body (as nicknamed by gossip rags) nee Bedi and Marc Robinson in a variety of *Kama Sutra*-esque poses.

The television commercial showed Pooja in a steamy shower sequence as Marc Robinson heads home to her. After much romancing of the head of the shower (of course) by her and much spraying of water, the voiceover informed you, 'KamaSutra Premium condoms. For the pleasure of making love.'

The sign-off was simple, 'Just ask for KS.'

The authorities did ask for KS – to be banned. Many television channels barred the commercial. Nevertheless, sales soared to, well, orgasmic heights and KamaSutra condoms became the top-selling brand in the country.

J.K. Ansell went on to supply the product to the Government of India and to NGOs for distribution in rural areas, and KamaSutra is still among India's most bought brands of condoms. A good position to be in after all.

To conclude, many brands court notoriety to gain mind-space, but not all of them do so coherently. 'True pleasure doesn't come in an instant,' we were told while being shown Arbaaz Khan and Malaika Arora in a suitably immodest pose. The product was Mr. Coffee.

Bisleri built up the action around a couple on a beach and then warned us to 'Play safe.' (By drinking their water, duh.)

Quite like 'item numbers', all these ads. And just like those songs, they can invite a lot of censure. Also if things don't go to plan, some ads swiftly go from bad press to facing an outright ban.

That Barnum guy who apparently said there is no such thing as bad publicity didn't really have a clue. Or did he?

After all, while some of these communication pieces get unwittingly caught in a hullabaloo, some of them actually just want the attention and are created with political incorrectness or titillation in mind.

Obviously these are not brands which are shy. Or which refuse to play, saying, 'Wham! Ban? No thank you, man.'

Character Loose

MASCOTS AT LARGE

'Loose *keraakter*!' Many a girl has muttered these words after encountering an oily-haired male singing a *besura 'Chal Chameli baag mein,'* equivalent as he brushes past.

'Inke khandaan ka character *theek nahin hai,'* my old neighbour would mutter while watching *Mahabharata* on television. She was basically dismissing the 'character' of all the fabled kings and queens (and fish) who were reproducing in and out of wedlock, often after eating the divine mango that fell in their laps. (Funny thing about fruit – in the Mahabharata there was a mango, in the Bible there was an apple – basically eating fruit makes *things* happen.)

The ad industry too is full of people whose characters are rumoured to be, well, a little *dheela*. However, the same cannot be said of some of the characters created by the industry. Tightly crafted, memorable characters not only populate the advertising landscape, but many are also part of popular culture. Gadding Gattu, the mustachioed Maharajah and savvy Lalitaji remain great examples of characterization.

Then among brand ambassadors, brand spokesmen and brand mascots, there is also the rabbit who likes *papad*, the beauty queen who has dandruff, the cricket team captain who likes batting his eyelashes and the iconic couple who get into action in the kitchen. They come into your home every day telling you what they think, eat, buy or shampoo their hair with.

Believe them or not, there they are.

Air India's Maharajah

Not so long ago, every down-and-out Maharajah and his minor relative started welcoming us into their modern *havelis* (but with authentically ancient foundations) in Rajasthan. *Firangi* tourists arrived by the busload, looking forward to waking up to a breakfast rendezvous with their royal hosts over *masala* chai and fresh orange juice (squeezed from Dabur tetrapaks).

Indira Gandhi may have snatched away the privy purse (that special *sarkari* allowance for being born in a *mahal* and not a hovel) from the ex-Maharajahs. But there was one Maharajah this didn't hurt: Air India's Maharajah.

Some would say it is this unaffected Maharajah who then showed the way that all royalty could have a career in serving people by becoming a part of the hospitality industry. Who better than the much-loved Maharajah mascot of Air India to demonstrate that a little bit of marketing smarts could help you expand your kingdom?

After all, before the 'Maharajah' became a McDonald's burger, before the hoi-polloi began buying discounted flight tickets and comparing ticket prices for air travel with those for trains – many tens of years ago, the Maharajah was Air India's mascot and an undisputed icon. At the time, flying on Air India was glamorous and exclusive. The inhabitants of that world were well-heeled passengers who were welcomed aboard by stylish flight attendants. Fitting right into this high-flying club, Air India's Maharajah personified the royal nature of a bygone era and the warmth of Indian hospitality. He was the exotic host transporting people to distant lands on his magic carpet. He was also cute, which the dictionary tells us is 'ugly but interesting'. The face of Air India's Maharajah was a total *chaudahveen ka chaand* – it was that round. He had a respectable paunch and his *mooch* stretched on for miles longer than his smile.

With these vital statistics, it is doubtful that he would have made even the stewarding grade. But his was the face that launched a thousand ships – up in the air.

The Air India story goes back to pre-independent India in the 1930s. One of Asia's largest companies at the time was Tata Sons Limited, of which J.R.D. Tata was a director. He created an aviation division, Tata Air Services, later renamed Tata Airlines, which he flagged off by taking the flight from Karachi (which was then a part of undivided India) to Mumbai (then Bombay) in 1932.[1] This marked the beginning of domestic air service in India.

The airline expanded over the years. In 1946, the company went public and the carrier was rechristened Air India Limited. Come 1948, the government of India acquired 49 per cent stake in the corporation. As the airline expanded, so did some other Indian domestic carriers –

---

[1] http://www.tata.in/aboutus/articlesinside/How-the-Maharaja-got-his-wings

Indian National Airways (INA) and Air Services of India (ASI) among them. There was a Bharat Airways as well, which had flights to places like Bangkok, Singapore and Hong Kong. Air India, too, had introduced services to London via Cairo and Geneva and, to cater to the large Indian presence in Nairobi, flights to the Kenyan capital via Aden in Yemen.

Meanwhile, with nationalistic feelings on the rise, there was a call for a single, national domestic airline, and in 1953, the government passed the Air Corporations Act, giving birth to two corporations. All the domestic carriers of the time were merged to form a single entity – the Indian Airlines Corporation – for domestic service. Air India International (abbreviated to Air India in 1962) got exclusive rights to fly internationally.

But let's go back to 1946 for a bit. India was still not independent then, and S.K. 'Bobby' Kooka was the commercial director at Air India. He knew that the small airline was competing with giants like TWA and Air France and needed to stand out somehow. While on a flight, he fiddled with the idea of using a monarch-like illustration on the company's letterhead – something like a Maharajah that would symbolize the warmth, exclusivity and Indian-ness he wanted the airline to be associated with.

Umesh Rao, who worked in the art department of the airlines' advertising agency J. Walter Thompson, was roped in to help. It was decided that the character would not be presented as a blue-blooded king, prince or princeling – he would only look regal. So Umesh Rao drew a quirky, turbaned figure who fit the bill.

Soon the Maharajah (blue-blooded or not, that was what he came to be known as) jumped out of the limits of letterheads. He started appearing in all the marketing material, by and by becoming synonymous with the airline. His uniquely Indian persona made him an instant mascot for Air India. When people thought of the Maharajah, they thought of Air India's hospitality (rather than the limited number of planes at the time) and vice versa.

The Maharajah was no snotty, uppity royal. He was an accomplished crowd-pleaser, a friendly guy bowing to welcome people to the experience of flying with Air India. People did not fly with Air India because it was the only Indian airline. They actually *liked* its service. The food was good, the staff was friendly and chic, and the Maharajah was oh-so-adorable.

He was the versatile guy who could give any stereotype a twist. He was the seller of naughty pictures in Paris and the drinks' server in a bottom-revealing dress in London. He was a monk, a street-side artist, an incorrigible flirt and a cancan dancer. Once, he was even the trophy on the wall as two tigers sat having a drink after a hunt. And when Tata had to give up their hold on the company, the Maharajah was roped in to try and maintain public confidence by telling, 'Tata does not mean bye-bye.'

In time, the mere presence of the Maharajah and the look of the communication told audiences that an advertisement was for Air India. In fact, some hoardings did not even carry the company's name, just carrying the Maharajah was enough. Very few airlines could – or still can – claim that distinction. Air India grew to be considered one of the most luxurious airlines in the world with a formidable reputation for good service.

Air India effectively used the Maharajah to its advantage. It incorporated his expressions, his puns and his activities into promoting its services and did this with a sense of humour that appealed to people. The Maharajah's wit and originality in communication won Air India many national and international awards.

However, the Maharajah's reign was not without controversy. In the 1980s, the Maharajah gained disfavour as he came to be perceived as an inappropriate feudal symbol in a country that was softly socialist. Air India responded to such concerns by removing him in 1989, but there was such a hubbub over this move that he was reinstated.

But even royal fortunes can change and Maharajahs can turn into relics. In the twenty-first century, the Maharajah's royal connections began to seem somewhat irrelevant. No longer seen as with-it, the Air India Maharajah saw himself reduced from a witty globe-trotter to a cardboard figure announcing flights.

Today, the airline itself is no longer the class act it used to be. The ageing Air India is in the headlines mostly for the wrong reasons. Routes that came with guarantees no longer rake in the money. Competition and politics have been taking centre stage in the Maharajah's realm.

But his legacy is the decades during which he ruled with his inimitable style and charm, not just as a symbol of warmth and hospitality, but as a very real person. In fact, the Maharajah still has his fans. This was obvious as recently as in 2014, when the company decided to make the Maharajah contemporary. It dressed him in jeans, spiked his hair and gave him a cellphone (of course) to slouch over. Fortunately, they kept his *mooch* intact.

Social media and the popular press erupted. They called the 'new guy' everything from a *sadak chhaap* Romeo to someone you expected would sleazily break into a song like, '*Aaja meri gaadi mein baith jaa...*' What a relief it was to be told that it was just one of the many avatars of the Maharajah, who continued to dabble with different looks.

It was simply a case of an old guy trying to fit in.

Asian Paints

There was a time in the 1950s when bathrooms were not temples of glamour. Indians often called it the very un-temple-like *gusal-khana*.

Yes, some also called it 'latrine'.

Walls used to be where you hung art from, not works of art themselves, and wall paints were certainly not an extension of your personality.

Har ghar kuch clearly *nahin kehta tha* and you never looked for *mera-wala* pink because you just said, 'Whitewash *waley ko bula lein?*'

Before paint played an important role in your life, and much before Sunil Babu got his *naya ghar* and *nayi gaadi*, Asian Paints got Gattu.

In the 1950s, paint was seen as a rather industrial product. The paints industry was peopled by big players and the Asian Oil and Paint Company was one of the small companies. But it always had chutzpah. Even today, when marketing stories about the old days get bandied around, the portrait of the Asian Oil and Paint Company is painted with admiration. People speak of how they began in a garage in 1942; how they had a turnover of ₹3.5 lakhs by 1945; how their marketing was a mix of innovative ideas, product development and distribution; how they gave a little boy a paintbrush and set him to work for them – and how they decided to call him Gattu.

In 1954, Asian Paints was looking for a way to define their brand in a more personalized way, giving it a customer-friendly persona. Cartoon characters as brand mascots or as design elements were the trendy marketing thing to do. Some of the blame for this lay squarely at the in-flight door of Air India, where you saw the Maharajah. The *Times of India*, too, had R.K. Laxman's 'Common Man', a character that people identified with immensely. Struck by the popularity of his creation,

Asian Paints reached out to Laxman and asked him to create a character for them as well.

The story goes that Laxman was smoking as he struggled to come up with an idea for the paint company. Through the smoke from his cigarette, he saw the likeness of a little boy holding a paintbrush in his hand. And just like that, out of thin air, came the inspiration of one of India's best-known brand mascots.

R.K. Laxman sketched a mischievous-looking boy with an unruly mop of hair, wearing the 'half-pants' many Indians were wearing those days. He was perfect, but he needed a name. So Asian Paints held a 'Give Me a Name' contest. Of the thousands of entries that came in, one name stood out (submitted by two different people – Mr Rele from Girgaum and Mr Aras from Sion) – and that's how the little boy, who did not grow up for decades and ubiquitously brought colour into many homes, came to be known by the unlikely name of Gattu.

From the 1950s to the 1970s, Gattu mischievously painted away, mostly in print ads. He would be seen doing things like painting a bald man's head while the line that supported his handiwork said, 'Any surface that needs painting needs Asian Paints.'

Things looked up for Asian Paints after Gattu was born. In the four years that followed, the company's sales are said to have gone up ten times. More importantly, Gattu made something as practical as paint, seen as a product that would interest only 'painters', transition into a category that drew in home-owners. Gattu wasn't always very funny or very lovable but he always got attention and helped command brand recall, transitioning paint from a low-interest product to one that appealed to the masses.

Familiar little Gattu became inseparable from the brand. In those years, no one could miss Gattu. Lovable and impish, he was a part of every Asian Paints communication. Even when he stopped being the hero of the ads, his presence was mandatory as an add-on in pre-approved styles and poses.

The new century brought with it new objectives for Asian Paints. No longer aiming only for the mass market, it set its sights on a premium tag. It moved from walls to other surfaces with a variety of finishes. As a company, it was no longer the manufacturer of cans of paint. Asian Paints was now a 360-degree solutions provider for the house-proud home-owner.

Once different brands and sub-brands were introduced for exteriors, interiors and even waterproofing, Gattu could no longer hold his own. Soon, the only place where he could be accommodated was on the product tins. Before he was phased out from Asian Paint's marketing campaigns, the company's powers-that-be asked to speak with R.K. Laxman. They felt they needed to explain to Gattu's creator why Gattu had to go. It is said that when told about Gattu's exit, R.K. Laxman did not seem overly concerned.

In 2015, when Laxman passed away, Gattu, with his trademark mop in place and dripping brush in hand, reappeared in the Asian Paints memorial ad dedicated to his creator. The ad said, 'For the one who saw every colour of life in black and white.'

Gattu irrevocably changed the market for wall paints, so much so that the entire industry has never looked back since.

Home-owners have long moved away from the days when a mundane 'whitewash' would suffice for the walls of their homes. They are now readily setting out on voyages of self-discovery and searching for the perfect colour and texture that will reflect their personal charm. (Although, after exulting over Tickled Pink and Wild Violet, the decision is often still a whitish colour, maybe glamorously called Whiter Wash or White Bright. But that is another tale.)

Surf

Who says home-makers mull over national budgets, global warming or nations at war?

If our ads are to be believed, the biggest concern for home-makers (read, women) in this country is the state of the daily laundry. That is, making sure that the family walks out in clothes washed brighter and whiter than the neighbour's.

In this mission, Surf has always assured the Indian woman that it is with her, and for her – always.

Surf was launched by Hindustan Lever Limited (now Hindustan Unilever Limited) in 1959. It was successful in the market, finding favour in homes all the way till the 1970s.

Then one day, out of the blue, it was noticed that the turf no longer belonged just to Surf. More and more people, it seemed, were lathering it up with a powder called Nirma. '*Sab ki pasand* Nirma!' went the jingle and for a while there even the revenue reports reflected that every 'Hema, Rekha, Jaya *aur* Sushma' was washing her dirty laundry with Nirma.

Launched by Karsanbhai Patel in 1969, in less than ten years, the washing powder started to pose a threat to the market-leader, Surf. That its price was just one-third that of Surf was definitely a factor and when Hindustan Lever realized it could not counter Nirma's popular price point, it decided to revive consumer interest in Surf by taking the route of value-consciousness. How it did this is a chapter fit for the history books.

Surf came up with Lalitaji – who showed up in a sparkling white sari and told everyone in a voice that commanded attention that there was a difference between a cheap product and a good product, between *sasti cheez* and *achhee cheez*.

The main character in a new campaign for Surf by Lintas, Lalitaji was conceptualized by Alyque Padamsee and his team and played by the actress Kavita Chaudhary.

No wallflower, she was the confident, clear-headed woman who made savvy choices. She did not give a *paisa* more than was warranted for anything she bought and made sure that the quality of what she bought was the best suited for her family. In short, Surf positioned itself as being priced higher than the average product simply because it was also the better one.

Lalitaji did not need approval; she did not seek advice. She had life under control and knew the good stuff when she saw it. At a time when women were depicted as voiceless creatures who allowed others (aka men) to take decisions on their behalf, here was a woman voicing her preferences with clear reasons of her own.

Before the ad was made official, the communication went through market research. The feedback on Lalitaji was not good. People found her irritating and didactic. In spite of that, a few key people on the marketing team at Levers and at the advertising agency believed in her persona and what she would do for the brand. They went with their gut and Lalitaji was unleashed on the country.

The television ads had a characteristic format. Lalitaji would be seen and heard doing something absolutely value conscious and typically middle class before she spoke to a never-seen-only-heard *Bhai-saab*, treating him as if he were slightly dense. To him, she would sternly and kindly explain all the pros of purchasing and using Surf.

In a typical ad, she could be seen bargaining with a *sabziwala*, or showing her child's shorts to the camera, talking about how she had got it altered so it could continue to be used. She would tell *bhai-saab* what a sensible thing she had done. Then she would go on to explain how buying Surf was just as sensible a thing to do.

The ads showed prudent facts for the budget-conscious homemaker who was also looking for quality products. One of these facts was that half-a-kilogram of Surf was equal to one kilogram of your average powder. This meant that one kilogram of Surf could wash twice the number of garments a kilogram of the average powder did – buying Surf was an economically sound decision as well as a quality choice.

Lalitaji quickly became a star and the face of one of Surf's most remarkable campaigns.

The mid-1980s were also the time when the television serial, *Rajani*, aired featuring an absolute crusader of a woman who did not hesitate to fight for her rights as a citizen of the country and as a person. These were startlingly fresh portrayals of women and they struck a chord with India's metamorphosing middle class.

Both characters have long since retired.

And though Lalitaji was no Ms Congeniality, she remains a definite winner in the memorability sweepstakes.

Onida

How many people did it take to watch television in India in the 1980s? The answer is three, boss. One to climb on to the roof and 'adjust' the antenna; one to fiddle with the knobs on the box; and one to be the go-between shouting, '*Thoda aur* left *ghumaao...bas! Arrey zyaada ghuma diya, yaar!*'

In 1982, when the Asian Games were held in India, the country was finally gifted the pleasures of viewing television in colour. So what if many of the films aired were still black and white? Or that many people owned black and white television sets? An enterprising few even attached screens with bands of blue, reddish-brown and green to make the black and white imagery look like sky, a middling-something and grass (Really, they did).

Families that did not own TVs gathered at a neighbourhood home that did own one to watch movies on Sunday, often of the *Mother India* vintage. It was a social occasion that warranted 'decent' clothes and maybe even some talcum powder dusted on the neck.

The live telecasts were significant as well. Indira Gandhi's funeral was watched by hordes squashed into drawing rooms across the country, commenting on the sorrow of the very handsome son, the beauty of the granddaughter and the unrealness of the assassination. 'So sad, *tch-tch*, look how nicely the *firangi bahu* (the one who hadn't been thrown out, you know) was wearing a sari.'

It didn't take long for the television to start appearing on the most-wanted lists of household items, and like other prized possessions in the 1980s, such as a scooter or a car, it was not a decision that was taken lightly.

Most customers looking to buy a television set were first-time buyers and very proud ones at that. This was no ordinary purchase. A colour television set made folks feel like they were a cut above the rest. There was a sense of having arrived – in fact, owning a remote-controlled television set ensured that the arrival lounge was of premium category.

Buying a television for your home needed research, particularly to decode the Japanese vs Indian vs other nationality genetics. The ancestry of a brand was important especially in relation to the television set at the neighbour's.

Onida was the result of a collaboration between JVC Japan and an Indian company, MIRC Electronics. The presence of some Japanese DNA in a brand was a *very* good thing. The trouble was, Onida entered the market late, so no one was scrambling to sing '*Le gaya dil,* TV *Japan ka...*' or anything to that effect. However, on the plus side, no established track record meant there was no looking back. Onida could only look forward.

Technology seemed to be the key to attracting consumers, so most brands communicated technical jargon to promote their products. When Onida entered the fray, there were already around 20 brands fighting it out in the market. The competition was among alien-sounding names like – Crowne, Salora, BPL, Dynora and Videocon.

BPL and Videocon were already doing well. But Onida had a huge advantage. They had over 60 channels as compared to the measly 10 or 12 channels most brands offered. (Never mind that there was only one Doordarshan to be depended on for televiewing fare.) Also, in those days when bulky CRT television sets looked like they were in serious need of a diet, Onida looked somewhat sleeker and flatter – another bonus for the brand.

Early on, Onida decided that joining the technology spewing bandwagon was not going to work. Instead, the opportunity lay in telling a good consumer-centric story. So it used its assets to sell a core emotion – envy. That is, if you wanted to make your neighbour jealous, you needed to get home an Onida TV. A television set was a status symbol and Onida was the first to advertise it this way. Accordingly, the slug line accompanying the ad was 'Neighbour's envy. Owner's pride.'

Now envy, we have always been told, is a sin. Who could sell a sin better than the devil? And so we got Onida's devil mascot, created by ad legend Gopi Kukde. The Onida devil was played by model co-ordinator David Whitbread. No one ever played the devil quite the way he did. His sharp, long, curved fingernails, his smooth head and his impish look are still remembered today.

In the early 1980s, Onida's television commercial featured a TV sitting in solitary splendour. Then *crash* – a stone was flung on its screen, smashing it. Clouds of smoke billowed all around and the devil's face peeped out from behind the TV just as you were told, 'Onida TV. Neighbour's envy. Owner's pride.'

The product itself getting destroyed? Blasphemy! But at the same time very noticeable. No one could ignore the devil either. His bushy eyebrows, ragged cloak and big tail were different from everything being advertised at the time. The line, too, caught everyone's fancy.

Presumably as a fallout of the ad, Onida's market share is estimated to have risen from 5–6 per cent in 1981 to 19–20 per cent in 1995.[2]

Over the next few years, the devil was given his due in ads. He became inseparable from the Onida communication till 1998, when it was decided that he needed to be given a break.

The choices available to Indian consumers after the economic liberalization had diminished the importance of 'envy' as an impetus for purchase. And though, in 2004, when the brand needed a boost, he was brought back with much optimism (and a contemporary feel), the magic was completely missing.

So in 2009, the Onida devil was finally laid to rest. Though, the day he stops being talked about as one of the most remarkable characters in Indian advertising is probably the day hell actually freezes over.

Parle-G

For decades now we have been dunking sweet Parle-G biscuits into sweeter chai while idly discussing the identity of the child featured on the iconic

[2] Subramanian, Samanth, 'A Devil of a Decision: Onida Mascot to RIP', *Livemint*, 10 September 2009

white-and-yellow-striped *biskut* packet. '*Woh kaun thi?*' we wonder.

For the longest time there was no consensus on who this girl was. Was is it even a girl at all? (Though the all-knowing ones did point out that it had to be a girl because of the Bollywood-heroine-inspired fringe, also known as the Sadhana-cut, which a whole generation of sadistic 1960s' mothers inflicted on their unsuspecting daughters. Plus the kid wore studs in her ears and as everyone knows, '*uss zamaane mein* boys earrings *nahin pehante the, rey*!')

Such is the curiosity inspired by the girl that question answer sites are, in fact, crawling with detectives claiming to possess definite knowledge of her identity.

'Revealed: The Parle-G girl is Sudha Murthy.'

'Just revealed: the Parle-G girl is Gunjan Gudaniya.'

'Finally revealed: Parle-G girl *badi ho kar* Airtel 4G girl *ban gayi hai*.'

Well, it turns out that the Parle-G girl is not a real girl at all, but an illustration created in the 1960s by the company's advertising agency, Everest Brand Solutions. The rest is all rumour and speculation. (Really? We've spent a lifetime speculating on an illustration?)

But that's not the important thing here. What is important is the sweet brilliance of Parle-G's branding and marketing. Whatever the age, education or mother tongue of the customer, he or she can identify the biscuit pack they want simply because of the familiar child on it.

Parle-G, or Parle Gluco, comes from Parle Products, which owns other biscuit brands like Monaco and KrackJack as well as confectionery brands like Melody, Mango Bite, Poppins and Kismi, among others.

Parle Gluco came into existence around 1939, about a decade after the Parle factory in Vile Parle in Mumbai (that's where the company's name was derived from) began producing confectionery like boiled sweets. Initially, they produced military-grade biscuits to supply to the British Army fighting in World War II, but eventually the Parle Gluco biscuits were also manufactured for local consumption. They were marketed as an affordable source of nourishment, and that is the positioning that Parle has more or less stuck to for decades.

During the British Raj, the other biscuits available were expensive – mainly imported brands like Jacob's Cream Crackers from United Biscuits, Huntly & Palmers biscuits and Glaxo glucose biscuit. Britannia, the other Indian biscuit-maker was based in Calcutta (now Kolkata), and while they were a name to reckon with in the eastern part of India, they did not manufacture glucose biscuits.

In the 1960s, by the time Britannia launched a rival glucose biscuit – Glucose D – there were already a number of other smaller players in the market, many producing glucose biscuits and some of them even producing knock-offs of Parle Gluco. Undiscerning customers would simply walk into shops asking for glucose biscuits, which had become a generic category among biscuits.

The need for a distinguishing factor prompted the Parle girl to make her first appearance. Created as an illustration by Maganlal Dahiya – a creative professional at Parle's advertising agency Everest Brand Solutions – the Parle girl with her chubby cheeks and large eyes, and wearing a white dress (which, incidentally, she hasn't changed out of in decades), was instantly liked by mothers and kids alike.

In 1982, Parle Gluco became Parle-G but the girl on its packaging remained constant along with other elements such as the font used for the brand lettering and the white and yellow stripes, though subsequently the stripes changed from horizontal to vertical and then to slanting.

Large-scale branding exercises helped tell consumers how Parle-G was 'often imitated, never equalled'. It stood out in every way, setting itself apart from biscuits sold in jars. For the customer, digging into a pack of Parle-G has always been about several, quite different things. Of course, Parle-G delivers on taste and nutrition and sometimes even works as a substitute for a meal or in keeping the customer mentally alert. But the crucial factor has always been its affordability as Parle-G's market is extremely price-sensitive and it is perceived as a value-for-money buy. Since a slight increase in pack prices can result in a temporary dip in demand, Parle has used in-house procurement and packaging solutions to help maintain prices which are still just a few rupees for small packs. This has helped them with market penetration, which in turn has played a vital role in its success and popularity. In 2012, its distribution network covered approximately six million retail stores across the country.

Today, the target audience for Parle-G is mainly six- to twelve-year-old kids and their mothers. But just like before, this biscuit still hits the sweet spots all around the bullseye. Parle-G is consumed by people across ages irrespective of income levels and social backgrounds.

The communication for Parle-G has always been about taste and strength. At one time, the endorser was the home-grown strongman and much-loved superhero, Shaktimaan. The brand has traditionally also done montages with jingles like, '*Swad bhare, shakti bhare, barson se*...Parle-G.' Then there was a 2003 campaign that embraced the consumer as part of a Parle-G-loving family that extended across the world.

By 2011, a study by the market research firm Nielsen proclaimed Parle-G to be the world's largest-selling biscuit brand.[3] It was said that if you laid every Parle-G biscuit consumed in a year, end to end, you would cover the earth's circumference over 190 times.

Value-for-money pricing, massive reach and a focus on the mass segment contributed to Parle-G's success. But a new generation of consumers and product options are now cutting into the demand for glucose biscuits. With

[3] Bhushan, Ratna, 'Parle-G World's No 1 Selling Biscuit: Nielsen', *Economic Times*, 3 March 2011

competition from brands like Britannia Tiger and ITC Sunfeast, Parle-G has been trying to hold on to its market share. To do this it has even tried to change tack, telling consumers that the 'G' really stands for 'genius' as the biscuit helps to stimulate intelligent curiosity.

Nevertheless, so iconic is the biscuit, with the *woh-kaun-thi* little girl on its packaging, that when the brand's first factory in Vile Parle was shutting down, a whole generation of Mumbaikars mourned that passing by that area would never be the same again without the familiar, delicious aroma of freshly baked Parle-G biscuits wafting through the air.

Even as the articles made the rounds, social media inhabitants with short attention spans eagerly began to post obituaries – for the biscuit brand, for their memories of the many hungry moments when the biscuit had come to their rescue and for the void that would now fill their days. Very few read the news in its entirety, which was that the chief cause for the factory shutting down was the lowered demand for the biscuits, not because the product was being discontinued. Parle-G biscuits would continue to be made elsewhere (at the same low price, mind you), and the kid who contributed so hugely to its popularity and success would live on – she is fine, thank you G.

Air Deccan

If your first flight took place many decades ago, it was probably on an Indian Airlines airplane and you will remember the flight attendants as gracious beings in rustling saris, who served you boiled toffees and sachets of 'scented paper' – towellettes moist with eau de cologne. Over the years, these beings seemed to have become constructed of sterner stuff, and some things may have changed service wise.

But by then, there were other options. You could always choose to fly with that 'other' airline where the attendants' smiles were sweet and the *imli* toffees were *khatta-meetha*.

When the Indian skies opened up in the 1990s following the deregulation of the Indian economy, a range of airlines made their appearance on the horizon. Damania Airways, EastWest, Jet Airways, Sahara, Modiluft and NEPC found themselves filling a much-needed space and began duding up to become household names. People who had grown up on Indian Airlines as the only domestic air carrier suddenly had other choices and in just a few years the new airlines had taken a major chunk of flyers under their wings.

However, the high-flying days did not last. By the late 1990s, one by one, Damania Airways, Modiluft, EastWest and NEPC all found themselves running into losses and being grounded. Jet survived and promising comfort and in-flight experience, it managed to grab the business end of the market – those flying on company expenses – and established itself as a name to contend with.

Meanwhile, the soon-to-be-famous Indian middle class was emerging as the subject of much scrutiny. It was clear that this tribe wanted to work hard and play hard. Travel was right up there on their wishlists. This was a great business opportunity and a new batch of airlines was born. Unlike the old names that lost the battle, these brands were eyeing the masses. It was the new millennium – there was a sense of optimism and things seemed to be in place for them to take off.

Air Deccan, India's first low-cost airline, was the one that led the way. Launched in 2003, it boasted no frills, no complimentary meals, nothing that could push up the price of the ticket into the unaffordable zone. Low-cost operations equalled low fares and that was the edge they had over the more established airlines. The one additional thing they offered was the romance of the promise made by Air Deccan's owner, Captain Gopinath: 'Now everyone can fly.'

A tear-inducing television commercial showed an elderly man thinking back to the time when, as a young man, he would take his son out on his bicycle. You saw him make a miniature wooden aeroplane inspired by a matchbox cover that he saw the boy clutching in his fist. Years later, the *daakiya* brings the man, now very much a senior citizen, mail from his grown-up son and announces to the village that the son has sent his father tickets – airplane tickets. And the old man goes to visit his son, flying with Air Deccan.

The commercial brought alive the accessibility of flying as an experience, in a way that every *paisa-*

conscious Indian could relate to. This was a nation where flying was a luxury only a few could buy into. So it was logical that when flight tickets were reasonably priced, there was a massive, untapped market just waiting to buy them. The potential was mind-boggling.

The common man was now ready to ditch the train and book a flight to any destination. And who better to champion this newfound access to the skies than a character already loved across the country, R.K. Laxman's Common Man?

The Common Man was R.K. Laxman's most-recognized work.

R.K. Laxman started working with the *Times of India* and various other newspapers in the 1940s. As a staff cartoonist, he would try to represent India and Indians by drawing frames featuring people from different states. Over time, with the pressure of deadlines mounting, he found himself dropping the state-specific characters and using one figure more and more often.

In his autobiography, *The Tunnel of Time*, published in 1988, Laxman describes the Common Man as a 'silent spectator' and writes about how the bespectacled, balding, scruffily moustachioed Common Man clad in a checked coat and dhoti had walked into his cartoons spontaneously, as if he had no hand in the character's creation.

Mostly sporting a bewildered expression, the Common Man never spoke. He was just there, observing and seemingly as confused as the rest of us about the state of the country, its development and the shenanigans of its politicians.

From 1951 onwards, he appeared every day in the *Times of India* comic strip titled *You Said It*. He was part of the morning chai-*biskut-akhbaar* ritual in households across the country and, over the years, became a celebrity in his own right. How many mascots can claim to have not one but two statues honouring them? The Common Man has one in Pune and another looking out at the sea in Mumbai.

In 1988, on the *Times of India*'s 150th anniversary, the Indian Postal Service issued a postage stamp with the image of the Common Man on it. Yes, the Common Man was a brand treasure, a muse and even an ad model.

R.K. Laxman had once done a cartoon with Air Deccan as its subject for the *Times of India*. In turn, Air Deccan found the Common Man to be the perfect match for its brand. After all, the idea behind establishing the airline was to enable the ordinary Indian citizen to afford an air ticket. It could be said that the Common Man was the inspiration behind Air Deccan in the first place.

Air Deccan contacted R.K. Laxman and requested his permission to use the character. The idea appealed to Laxman as his lifelong belief had been that the common man needed to live a better life. In 2005, not only did he give Air Deccan permission to use the character as their brand ambassador, he also did not charge them anything.

For Air Deccan, which signed off with 'Simply fly', it was a coup of sorts. One of the most recognizable figures in the country was now going to be in their hangar. It was decided that the mascot would not just be visible in airports and the company's brand communication but also be painted on the aircraft, both inside as well as outside. To bring alive the association and to get itself closer to its target market, in 2005 Air Deccan came up with a promotional offer of tickets for just ₹1 which could be booked 90 days in advance. There was fine print to be read too, of course: Every Air Deccan Airbus would offer four or five seats at this price. There were also fares as low as ₹500 and 40 per cent of the seats were priced below ₹2,500.[4]

The result? Demand for flight tickets grew fast, especially because of the throwaway fares.

Around three years after Air Deccan began its operations, it had a fleet of 43 aircrafts and serviced over 350 flights a day, covering about 65 airports.[5] Its fleet boldly went where other airlines had feared going before – Tier 2 cities, where the aspirations of the people translated into flight tickets. But its rapid growth was accompanied by complaints about its service being unpunctual and undependable. Among other things, fast expansion into routes that were not viable resulted in losses for the airline.

Meanwhile, bigger, older players like Indian Airlines, Jet and Sahara took a page from Air Deccan's book and started discounting their fares.

---

[4] 'Air Deccan Unveils New Mascot', *The Hindu*, 5 May 2005

[5] Dey, Sudipto, 'Making Flying a Common Man's Word', *Economic Times*, 1 June 2007

In 2007, the Vijay Mallya-owned Kingfisher Airlines acquired a stake in Air Deccan. It was like mixing Scotch with *shikanji*. Kingfisher was flashy and upscale, promising its flyers 'good times'; while Air Deccan had always been simply about flying.

With the acquisition the rebranding of Air Deccan began. The name of the airline was changed to Simplyfly Deccan, its blue and yellow colours were changed to the more flamboyant Kingfisher red which also became the new colour of the flight attendants' skirts. And even though they consolidated their might, by November 2009, Kingfisher Airlines reported a net loss of ₹418.77 crore during the second quarter of the fiscal year.[6]

Expectedly, the airline did not last. Today, even as the Indian Airlines Maharajah dodders, his challenger, the 'king of good times' has been exiled. There is still much admiration, though, for the Captain (slated to be making a comeback) who dreamed of enabling every Indian to take a flight at least once in his or her lifetime and created a disruption in the Indian aviation industry.

As for the common man taking a flight, a slew of discounted airlines have made sure that it is not so uncommon any more.

[6] 'Kingfisher Airlines Crisis: Timeline', *The Hindu*, updated 13 June 2017

Patanjali

'Baba, black sheep.'

'*Yogi, bhogi, dhongi.*'

'Baba in the boardroom.'

For the longest time, Baba Ramdev has been called all kinds of names, but like the proverbial differently coloured sheep, he has chosen to go his own way, to follow his passion rather than the herd.

In a world obsessed with parading scantily-clad women in ads for all kinds of products, Baba Ramdev has shown that a scantily-clad man, too, can sell products. From talking the talk (which is what all gurus can do) to performing yogic contortions (that only some of them can do), he has evolved into what very few of them can become – the man behind a business empire that some predict could be the biggest success story in India's fast-moving consumer goods sector.

When it comes to marketing, this baba is no timid lamb, and as his operating style reveals, he is not leading sheep either. Though when, a decade or so ago, he was showcased on channels named along the lines of 'Devotion' – there sat the masses hanging on to his every move. When he stretched his limbs, they did too. When his nostril flared, taking in a deep breath, theirs did the same. When his belly was drawn in forcefully, their collective bellies, umm...wiggled aspirationally. When he laughed out loud, they laughed too. Today, with his following becoming bigger and bigger, the Baba is still laughing the loudest.

Long known for his mass yoga camps and for propounding the ancient medicinal wisdom of Ayurveda, Baba Ramdev teamed up with an Ayurvedic expert, Acharya Balkrishna to set up a small pharmacy by the name of Patanjali Ayurved Ltd (PAL), inspired by no less a person than the legendary father of yoga and cleverly combining two health practices in its name.

While Balakrishna is said to own a 92 per cent stake in the company[7], an expatriate owns the rest. Surprisingly, Baba Ramdev does not hold any stake in the company. Founded in 2006, the company's manufacturing units and headquarters are in Haridwar while their registered office is in Delhi.

The competition for Patanjali's products has been around for ages. Companies like Baidyanath, Vicco and Dabur espouse similar values and manufacture products with Ayurvedic formulations. To cater to their specific market, they have for long invested in advertising their brand value and their company heritage, not to speak of the unique character of their products.

Patanjali began with none of this in place. It was a newcomer in the segment and the only visible icon it

---

[7] Rai, Saritha, 'An Indian Yoga Guru's Consumer Products Brand, Patanjali, is Making Global and Domestic Rivals Sweat', *Forbes*, 15 October 2015

had was Baba Ramdev. As it turns out, that was more than enough. From the beginning, the bearded baba had crowds eating out of his hands.

Patanjali's range of food products has shown an impressive expansion. They even have products that have become familiar but sound foreign. In addition to this, they manufacture and sell Ayurvedic formulations of all the normal grocery-list items, toothpastes and soaps, gels and shampoos, and so on. With Ayurvedic and traditional food products, the company has practically taken on the might of Hindustan Unilever Limited, Nestlé, Procter & Gamble, to name just a few.

In a coup of sorts, a tie-up with the mammoth Future Group owned by the industrialist Kishore Biyani has ensured that Patanjali Ayruved products occupy pretty solid *asanas* on the shelves of supermarkets such as Big Bazaar and Nilgiri.

But if there is one baba conquering the boardroom, can others be far behind? Looking at his success, more baba-*log* are now joining the fray and Patanjali (and the FMCG biggies) may just see new competition emerging from Sri Sri Ravi Shankar, Sadhguru Jaggi Vasudev and others.

Patanjali has always been clear about its path as a brand. It claimed to stand against the disguised agendas of MNCs and the nature of their products, pointing to the hidden menace of chemicals, the obvious exploitation of farmers and big corruption in their competitors' backyards. Patanjali tried telling us what we had always suspected was true: We need to be suspicious about what we are consuming.

Their operations and distribution set-up too reflected their thinking. If you wanted to deal in Patanjali products, you could fill an online form. You needed to declare yourself a supporter of the movement that was committed to making the country self-reliant and an economic superpower. As dealers *and* consumers, you were pledging your commitment then and there. Yes, you were sort of in the army now. You were definitely part of a movement.

While the nationalistic spin appealed to some people, others opted for Patanjali because they felt it was the healthier option among those available. Still others were just part of the ever-growing Baba Ramdev fan club. But, overall, more and more people became willing to try Patanjali products as the products appeared on shelves in markets across the country.

The products, by virtue of focusing on the 'natural' aspect, skyrocketed in perception as being 'better' in some way. Added to this was the word-of-mouth publicity about the quality of the products. There were fervent testimonials to the purity and wonder of Patanjali's products. To these goodwill ambassadors, Patanjali could have said, '*tumhaare moonh mein ghee-shakkar*,' and it would not have seemed just slick talk. Because Patanjali Ghee is among the products that have received the most positive endorsements.

In their packaging, Patanjali products often target the competition quite clearly.

There may have been some unmet expectations among some consumers but mostly the sentiment was that the 'feel' of most Patanjali products, if not better, was at the very least similar to products that had already been tried. In addition, many Patanjali products were also priced cheaper than their market counterparts. Where the aura of 'natural goodness' around their products makes most brands indulge in a good bit of *nakhra* and become pricier, here was one brand that displayed a similar halo and at a much lower price.

To make things even better, the distribution of the products was phenomenal. Much like the Baba's believers, the products were to be found everywhere – in big towns, in small *gullies*, in villages, and on online portals.

The flexible and mobile structure of the organization has worked well for Patanjali. Along the way, advertising was stepped up and in the last week of November 2016, the brand was one of the top three brands advertised on television (as per the Broadcast Audience Research Council [BARC]).[8]

And there's certainly no dissing the appeal of their brand ambassador. Baba Ramdev is no Kareena or Katrina but his items do deliver numbers. And a lot of it is because

---

[8] Rukhaiyar, Ashish, 'Patanjali Products Find a Growing Market', *The Hindu*, 3 February 2016

of his huge following as there is complete resonance between his teachings and the features of his products.

While competing directly with established players in the country, Patanjali is also going *saat samundar paar*, taking on players in other markets. With herbal alternatives and yoga having a distinct appeal in the West, the products are being exported to Canada, the US, Mauritius and the UK, among others, Patanjali clearly hopes to cash in on the 'back to nature' aspect and the positioning of their products as 'exotic' items made from ancient formulations.

From revenues of ₹450 crore in the fiscal year 2012, Patanjali recorded an increase to ₹5,000 crore in the fiscal year 2016[9] and a reported turnover of over ₹10,000 crore in the fiscal year 2017.[10]

Then there's all the buzz even on social media. Brand Patanjali generated over 15,000 conversations on Twitter in the second half of 2015.[11] The chatter was around its competitiveness, the quality of its products and its marketing strategy. At the end of 2016, Baba Ramdev himself had 6,44,000 followers on Twitter and 77,06,728

---

[9] Gupta, Pankaj, Deepak Himan and Vasant Ramadoss, 'The Secret Behind Patanjali's Rise and Rise', *The Hindu Business Line*, 3 November 2016

[10] Wadhwa, Puneet, 'Is Patanjali's Rs 20,000 Crore Revenue Target Realistic? Experts Weigh In', *Business Standard*, 5 May 2017

[11] According to data compiled by social media analytics firm Blueocean Market Intelligence. Chaturvedi, Anumeha, 'Brand Patanjali Driving Buzz on Social Media', *Economic Times*, 16 March 2016

likes on his page on Facebook.[12] Enough to get the MNCs' knickers into a knot.

As for the baba, his knicker/*dhoti* is knotted neatly and his beard seems to defy gravity, even when he twists into an impossible pose.

Vodafone

Way back in the 1940s, we were so entranced by the notion of a phone call that we could sing a whole song about a *piya* who went to Rangoon and called up on a '*taileefoon*'.

Some decades later, there was still romance around receiving a phone call. The 'trunk' call was a very significant thing, made more of an event by the long waits involved (in connecting), crackle in the 'line', and the often abrupt call drops. Not to mention the whole family excitedly gathered around the receiver, eager to do an immediate post-mortem of the now-fully-dead call.

It was a zoo out there, right up till the 1990s.

Then for a while, in more recent years, it became a zoozoo out there. We had graduated to cellphones and now were being charmed by Spielbergian creatures who were brand spokespersons and talked in snorts and grunts.

Remember the zoozoos? Those white humanoids, the ones that inhabited a parallel world? The ones that

---

[12] Narayanan, Chitra, 'Baba Ramdev: The Social Media Sanyasi', *The Hindu Business Line*, 29 December 2016

had cute ways of illustrating how Vodafone would make things better for us in every way?

They were noticed widely and commanded much affection. In fact, it was quite a black and white (and fifty shades of grey) case of love at first sight.

The story begins with Hutch, short for the Hutchison Asia Telecom Group. In the early 2000s, the cellular company grabbed consumer attention with ads featuring a *cho-chweet* boy and his ugly-as-sin-but-adorable pug. Just like the dog which solemnly followed the boy ALL the time – including to the classroom and to the barber's – Hutch told us it was with us *everywhere*. 'Wherever you go, our network follows.' (Stalker alert, anybody?)

Then Vodafone, one of the leading telecom brands in the world, came along and acquired a majority stake in what was by now a Hutchison-Essar joint venture, and in 2007 Hutch was re-branded as Vodafone. In India, the pug was still very strongly identified with Hutch. To superimpose its brand identity on that of Hutch, Vodafone went through a communications exercise where it played around with imagery incorporating the pug but also illustrating how the brand had changed. 'Wherever you go, our network follows,' was thus replaced with 'Make the most of now'.

But as time went on, being a basic telecom services provider meant being just one among a herd of players. Providing facilities was not just about voice calls and SMS anymore – there were many factors at play. There were other companies which were leading in related segments like CDMA or, among other things, in terms of the number of subscribers. Players like Airtel, RCom, BSNL, Idea Cellular, Aircel, Tata DoCoMo and MTNL were vying for the consumer's attention. To help them in their task were their brand ambassadors – Hrithik Roshan, Deepika Padukone, Abhishek Bachchan, Mahendra Singh Dhoni and others.

A stream of new entrants meant everyone had to lower tariffs to stay in the game, thereby reducing revenues. This in turn led to a need to develop alternative streams of revenue in order to thrive. Therefore, voice calls and SMS services aside, Vodafone wanted to showcase its innovative side and be taken seriously as a major presence in the Indian telecom industry. To be perceived as an entity bigger than a basic communications provider, it decided to promote its Value-Added Services (VAS).

Playing on the needs of the new consumer who was interested in using the mobile phone for personal expression, was a smart move. Mobile phones had become status symbols and were seen as extensions of the users' personalities. This insight – that a mobile device could be used for self expression and interests – opened up new possibilities. You could, for instance, have a caller tune that you thought reflected something about you or your state of mind. The idea was to achieve high recall, and in order for that to happen Vodafone decided to move beyond things like connectivity, clarity or low tariff and become inextricably linked to being *the* provider of VAS.

The opportunity arose with the arrival of the mega-cricketing event: the 2009 Indian Premier League (IPL). This – one of the biggest mass-involvement, mass-media properties in India – provided Vodafone with an audience that held massive potential. Vodafone wanted a 360 -degree marketing campaign that could be carried through the cricket series. It wanted to show off a range of VAS features and benefits to its customers – messaging, games, pictures, ringtones, information services, bill-payment options and Vodafone Live which was its multimedia portal service.

And that is when the zoozoos came into being. The idea was to create characters who would be quirky in look and manner, and deliver the message in a clutter-breaking way. After much experimentation, the characters chosen were all-white with large black dots for the eyes and the mouth. The heads resembled eggs and the bodies were unexpectedly thin. And they didn't seem to believe in sucking in their breaths so they had the bellies of the prosperous.

Meanwhile, the venue for the IPL had moved to South Africa. With less than a month to execute the campaign before the IPL began, the ad agency's film crew also shifted to South Africa. There, the ads were shot with South African actors wearing white, balloon-like quirky costumes. Yes, they were humans who wore costumes that made them look egg-headed. When they were finally seen, however, the characters did give rise to some debate over whether they were animated figures or real ones.

To keep the figures looking thin and small, the actors chosen to play them were mostly women and sometimes children. They were dressed in costumes which were stuffed with foam in places to give them the trademark look. In comparison, the egg-shaped heads were hard and gigantic. The ads were shot against a grey background that would not take attention away from the characters. An additional quirk was the zoozoos' speech – it was gobbledygook and entirely unintelligible.

Twenty-five ads featuring the zoozoos were shot in just ten days. Each television commercial showed the zoozoos interacting with each another, telling a simple product story. The first ad in the series was the one for phone backups. A whole queue of zoozoos were seen standing in line to get their faces photocopied in a photocopier, the takeaway being that Vodafone allowed the creation of a backup for the entire phonebook. The other ads were for offerings like cricket alerts, IPL contests, musical greetings, beauty alerts, call filters, Vodafone maps and live games, among others.

Mostly seen during the telecast of the IPL, the curious characters were an instant hit. People began asking what they were called and the nonsensical name 'zoozoos' seemed to fit the bill. It was fun-sounding, rolled off the tongue easily and was memorable and catchy. What's more, the characters served to illustrate that the Vodafone experience would be different with products and services that added convenience to the consumers' activities.

A few months after the zoozoos were first seen on television, they got their own merchandise, appearing on T-shirts, clothes, mugs, bed furnishings, and so on. Since the speed with which content is refreshed on social media was a critical factor, the company not only uploaded the making of the commercials but also developed 'Tag Me' applications, puzzles, dodgeball games, a caption contest and polls.

The zoozoos were here to stay. *Hum paunchy ek daal ke:* that could have been their anthem song as they continued to delight viewers season after season. In 2012, responding to feedback that they had perhaps overstayed their welcome and that youthful audiences were ready for a change, Vodafone did not release zoozoos' ads for a whole year.

When they did return in 2013, they came back as a whole army of mini zoozoos to a rousing welcome. Soon, they had almost two crore people engaging with them on Facebook, proving that there still was something to the creatures.

The zoozoos were the perfect partner for Vodafone's rebranding strategy in India and helped the brand showcase its transition from a basic communication services provider to a VAS provider. But the celebrities they created, the zoozoos, became stronger than the service itself. So while the overall experience may have been a mixed bag for Vodafone, the zoozoos themselves secured the top spot in consumer memory.

Not least for the memorable ways the pronunciation of their name changed across the country, depending on where/who you were – *Joojooj*, *Jhoojjus*, even (sweet *Jeejus*, we kid you not) *Sooosoos*.

To conclude, brand spokespersons add a lot to our product interactions. If you are feeling neither shaken nor stirred by life, you can soon be. All you have to do is watch a certain ad.

It shows a man taking over your field of vision. This is no ordinary man. He is the man whom God himself created to fit a suit. He has traversed the globe, taking on villains, taking up with vamps and coming out of the experiences not just alive (that is so *ordinary*) but oozing sex appeal. Today, though, he who once called himself Bond, James Bond, is holding up a tin of Pan Bahar.

'Class never goes out of style,' Pan Bahar's newest brand ambassador, Pierce Brosnan, tells you.

C-h-e-w o-n t-h-a-t, p-e-o-p-l-e.

We may not have exported a James-Bond-playing actor to Hollywood but we may have imported a James-Bond-playing actor who is possibly not averse to singing, '*Khaike paan* Benares-*wala*!'

But before human beings became popular as mascots and brand ambassadors, animals were all the rage. Smiling Shera was the lion king of the XIX Commonwealth Games held in 2010 in New Delhi. Representing majesty, courage, power and grace, he invited participation in the games, calling people to, 'Come out and play.'

Cadbury's Gems used to have cute, colourful pandas doing the talking for them. These guys would do anything to get their paws on Gems just like so many kids would. What's more, they would change colour on eating the Gems, and different pandas were promoted in different television commercials. The campaign's line, '*Raho umar*less,' genuinely got people of all ages collecting, swapping and posting pictures of their panda characters on social media.

Back in the dreary, un-cuddly world of humans, who can forget Chintamani? In 2005, Chintamani began as the mascot of ICICI Prudential Bank. He was a claymation character who stood out in the competitive clutter that made up the advertisements of the insurance industry. Middle-class, middle-aged Chintamani was a worried man looking out for good investment opportunities. He may have tapped into the depressive streak in all of us – the one that makes us turn to insurance companies so we can be happy at the thought of dying. Such was the popularity of Chintamani that though he was originally meant only for radio, he soon started appearing in television commercials, too.

But before the worry-wart became a mascot, happiness was found in another one – the Boomer Man. In the 1990s, Boomer Man was the candylicious superhero who exhorted you to chew on a Boomer. In the chewing-gum market, Boomer Man may just have been the reason Boomer chewing gum flew to the top. Not only did he save the day in the television commercials, he endorsed his own set of merchandise – temporary tattoos and stationery being popular items among them.

Appu, the lovable mascot of the 9th Asian Games held in 1982, is probably the first brush most Indians had with a line-drawn home-grown mascot. Modelled on a six-year-old elephant called Kuttinarayanan, Appu not only had a fan following but also got himself matchbox covers and even had a whole theme park dedicated to him. Not many mascots can match that.

Going back to even earlier times, we would stare at the dog staring at the gramophone on RCA records (you know, the things we used to play scratchy, wonderful music with, and now the things that kids want to play Frisbee with?). The intriguing *firang* mascot was based on an 1899 painting titled 'His Master's Voice', the real-life model for which was a dog called Nipper. The title of the painting is also where the record company HMV got its name, and the melody-loving dog is intrinsic to most of the musical memories from those years.

Somewhere in brand ambassador/mascot land, you can imagine Nipper the dog still listening to his master's voice while Appu romps with Chintamani. The Nirma girl shakes a leg, the Twitter blue bird flutters overhead (watch out for flying bird poop!), and the hills are alive with the sound of errm...music (...or is that the Airtel ads' signature tune?).

It is an interesting kind of place. Here, if you have something to say, you can find just about the right rabbit, housewife, cricket captain or oddball to say it with (or for you).

Creating memorable characters, tunes, ideas and images is what brands do to engage consumers and have audiences eating out of their hands. And audiences often oblige...until the cricket team captain leads India to defeat in a tournament. Then there's a chance that his house will get stoned and channels will be changed when he appears in an ad – because no one can STAND the sight of him. And when audiences turn away from the mascot, it can take its toll on the brand too.

The thing is, brands often invest big in 'the one' – their ambassadors. And they hope that for their audiences, these characters will be above reproach and more than just a nit-picky romance. That is, their man/woman/cross-dresser will always bring in the votes. And (of course) the notes.

Thoo-Thoo, Main-Main

BRANDS FIGHT THOOTH 'N' NAIL

Tyuuuuuuuung!!
Main samay hoon...

Thus would begin BR Chopra's TV serial, *Mahabharat*, a cult classic for anyone who was alive (and awake) on Sunday mornings in the 1980s. It was cult because everyone and their neighbour watched it in community silence. You cursed the duffer on the roof twiddling the antenna if you didn't get 'signal' by the appointed hour, when it was *samay* to go '*tyuuuuuuung*'.

It was also a classic because, even today, many remember the long drawn-out episodes of the battle, when brothers in armour started throwing weapons like *astras*, *asuras* and even *apsaras* at each other and shot *teer pe teer*, arrows which sometimes took two entire episodes (and, therefore, nine whole days to reach the target).

And what arrows!

They flew (for those nine days) looking, for all the world, like an early Diwali *fooljhadi* that had decided to get airborne. Some of those arrows could even make wind (uncontrollable apparently, and with not a hint on anybody being constipated).

The audience watched enthralled even though they knew the outcome of the war.

Chopra's sway with the audience could make some marketers very envious as they get into their very own mega (and mini) battles with other's brands. In this, they employ weapons like guerilla marketing, the odd hit-and-run and sometimes plain old defamation.

While the Cola Crusades are acknowledged epics, the battlefield of marketing is littered with many corpses from skirmishes for territory, for mind space and for the crown.

Truly, this is stuff well worthy of popping open that bag of popcorn and settling in for a watch – except that it is the audience itself which is in the crosshairs.

In the last few centuries, much of the world was colonized by Europeans with a mission – convert heathen folk to purer, 'White-r' ways. Today, this mission, as every lathering product will tell you, is indisputably the Indian housewife's.

Not only does she have to ensure that her family wears *pyore*-white and goes out dressed to dazzle but also that they do so after dining off shiny, sparkling steel...umm... *kadahis*. We are talking about *chakmak safai* here, *jagmag* even, and of late with zero *keetanu* (all brutally murdered during the said *safai*).

'Thou shalt not love thy neighbour,' brands tell you, encouraging you to twinkle, twinkle a little brighter than your *padosee*. They work hard to make you shine – they compete, compare, analyse, strike surgically and tattle on each other.

The mother of all these battles could well be the one between Lalitaji and Deepikaji, two memorable women who took up cudgels on behalf of *behatar safedi* in the 1980s.

Surf's Lalitaji launched an ad war on Nirma, a brand that sold at one-third the price of Surf. She claimed it didn't provide the better *safai* that her Surf did. To smite her, Deepikaji entered another shop (and ad), wanting the best *safedi* at *kam daam* with, what else, Nirma Super.

The soap operas had begun.

And while some of them could still be playing out, we end most of the episodes below just before a 'court scene'.

Ezee vs Safewash

'I*nhee* logo *ne le lee na...*' could well have been the complaint in this case. Because it was the brand logo which became the victim of comparative advertising.

In 2007, a print ad for Wipro's Safewash showed a mother and baby wearing woollens, accompanied by the headline, 'Wipro Safewash *hai* Ezee *se behtar*.' Instead of the word, Ezee, the headline had the Ezee logo itself.

Below the image was a chart, pointing out that Safewash contained neem while Ezee did not. It also said that the 500 ml pack of Safewash was 'effectively' priced at ₹45 while the same quantity of Ezee was priced at ₹66.

Godrej Consumer Products Ltd's (GCPL's) claim was that Ezee was the market leader in the liquid detergent category. The comparison between ingredients and pricing apart, Godrej found the use of Ezee's logo a legal violation.

It took matters to court on the grounds that Wipro's ad was 'disparaging and was misleading the consumer'.

Rin vs Tide

A guaranteed way to start a fight is by 'name-calling', even if it just about calling out your rival's name in an ad in a not entirely complimentary way.

In 2010, while Procter & Gamble (P&G) advertised its newly-launched product Tide Naturals (launched in December 2009), the competition, namely Hindustan Unilever Limited (HUL) decided to nip the product's blossoming in the bud itself.

Even as Tide's first commercial was doing the rounds, HUL moved court and, in March 2010, got Tide Naturals to admit that the ingredients were synthetic.

That same month, they released a television commercial for their product – Rin – that bore the distinction of being one of the few ads in which a brand actually took the name of a competing brand (namely Tide) and made a direct comparison.

The television commercial opened on two mothers waiting at the bus stop for their kids to come home from school. Both women were carrying shopping baskets. One woman's basket held a pack of Rin while the other's had Tide Naturals. The latter mentioned her purchase, talking about Tide's *'khushboo aur safedi bhi'*.

When the school bus arrived with the two children, the Tide-boy emerged wearing a meh-white shirt but (quick, where are the sunglasses?) the Rin-boy made his entry, dressed to blind in a shirt that was fiercely and ferociously white. Yes, the plot had taken a dark turn.

Running past the shocked Tide-Aunty to his very own Rin-Mummy, he asked, 'Aunty *chaunk kyon gayi?*', referring to the punch line in the Tide commercial, '*Chaunk gaye?*'

The ad concluded that Rin gave *behatar* whiteness at a *chaunkane wala* price of ₹25, even as a super further informed you that the ad was 'Issued in the interest of Rin users'.

Well, time and Tide wait for none. Tide detergent's manufacturer P&G filed a case against the Rin advertisement from HUL. HUL too challenged P&G's claim that Tide provided whiteness with a special fragrance. It insisted that the Rin commercial was in line with advertising regulations and that its claims were *factual-and-substantiated-by-laboratory-tests-under-globally-accepted-protocols-in-independent-third-party-laboratories-phew*.

A good fight always attracts an audience and soon rumours began doing the rounds. Was Rin losing market share and was this a desperate ploy to stop its decline? Or was Rin simply being smart by taking away Tide Naturals's shine before it established itself?

Some were of the opinion that the instance might even spark a new trend – that of releasing advertising campaigns which would serve a controversial purpose. By the time the controversialists got pulled up the damage to the competing brand would be complete.

You could always say 'sorry *ji*' later.

Vim vs Dettol Kitchen

There are probably more germs on your kitchen counter than on your potty-seat. This and (f)*ewww* other facts like this are brought to you by Big Companies as they fight it out for rights over your personal germs.

In 2013, the liquid dishwashing soap segment was estimated to be close to ₹300 crore, which was about 15 per cent of the overall dishwashing market that includes bars, powders and liquids. Growing at a rapid 40 per cent, the liquid segment was the fastest growing among dishwashing formats.[1]

Vim, from HUL, had dominated the dishwashing space in India for almost a century. In 2013, Reckitt Benckiser (RB) launched Dettol Kitchen, positioning it as a 'complete kitchen cleaner'. Things got dirty when the launch commercial for Dettol's dishwashing and kitchen-cleaning gel *showed* the Vim dishwash liquid while comparing the two products.

The film opened on two germ-infested plates, with teeny-tiny *keetanu* crawling all over. It went on to show how the plate that was cleaned with Dettol became germ-free, while the germs still remained on the one that was cleaned with Vim. To reiterate the point being made, a message at the bottom of the screen said, 'Compared to leading dishwash liquid, based on lab test.'

---

[1] Gurtoo, Himani Chandna, 'A War For Your Kitchen', *Hindustan Times*, 8 July 2013

In retaliation, Vim released a front-page print ad in a leading newspaper asking people whether they would choose a harsh antiseptic to clean their child's tiffin-box or the power of 100 lemons (the ingredient they claimed Vim contained). 'No one removes grease better. No one removes germs better. That's a Vim challenge!' said the ad. Simultaneously, Vim took the matter to court and so did RB's Dettol, challenging Vim's print ad.

But the consensus seemed to be that whatever the verdict, the damage to Vim had already been done. After all, germ-slaying was a long-established virtue of the Dettol mother-brand and Dettol Kitchen had capitalized on that.

Dettol Antiseptic vs Lifebuoy Total Soap

Not content with washing their dirty dishes in public, HUL and RB decided to take the fight to the bath.

In 2012, the health soaps market was worth around ₹3,000 crore. In this, HUL's Lifebuoy had around a share of 15 per cent, while Dettol soap – with its upmarket identity – was priced higher than Lifebuoy and had an 8.2 per cent share.[2]

Both Dettol and Lifebuoy also had product extensions like handwashes and hand sanitizers. Dettol, with its trusted germ-killer positioning was also the leader in

[2] Pinto, Viveat Susan, 'In War of Germs, Dettol and Lifebuoy Enter Round Two', *Business Standard*, 16 March 2013

the antiseptic liquids market, which was estimated to be around ₹150–₹200 crore. [3]

It is well-known that the germ-protection turf is much fought over by brands who occupy the health platform, but when Lifebuoy *Soap* took on Dettol Antiseptic *Liquid* by making a direct comparison, people did a double-take. It seemed like the equivalent of comparing apples and *ajwain*.

The print ad was divided into two halves, representing the effect of the cleaning done by the two products and clearly showed the Dettol part had more germs left after cleaning, indicating that Lifebuoy soap delivered better germ protection than Dettol Antiseptic Liquid.

The copy went on to explain that the effectiveness was about germ-protection (in tiny font size the ad said 'while bathing'), which – according to the dilution norms specified on the Dettol Antiseptic Liquid bottle – was one teaspoon in a bucket of water.[4]

Apparently 'Public *sab jaanti hai*,' but does not know that taking a bath with some Dettol liquid thrown in may not be enough. Which is maybe why the Lifebuoy ad also said it was 'issued in public interest'.

Since Dettol Antiseptic Liquid is where Dettol derives its glorious germ-slaughtering reputation from, Reckitt Benckiser could not let this pass. A complaint was made

[3] Ghose, Jayati, 'Liquid Dettol Price Likely to Rise as Pharma Dept Orders Review of Price Cap', *Financial Express*, 13 August 2013

[4] Menon, Rashmi, 'Round Two: Now Lifebuoy Attacks Dettol', *afaqs!*, 12 March 2013

and that is how a matter of bathing became a matter for the courts.

Dettol Soap vs Ayush

Yet another time that Reckitt Benckiser had to fight to defend its reputation as the most effective germ-slayer in the Indian market was in 2003, when the brands in contention were HUL's Ayush soap and RB's Dettol soap.

A television commercial for Ayush opened on a pregnant woman in a train. She needed help and a doctor was aiding her. When the doctor asked for hot water and soap, someone handed her a suspiciously familiar-looking soap. The doctor rejected it saying that in a situation like the one they were in, you didn't just need an antiseptic, you needed a protector. HUL's Ayurvedic soap, Ayush, was then shown as a body '*rakshak*', a protector, the first Ayurvedic soap to remove seven kinds of germs and provide protection against infection.

Claiming that HUL was undermining Dettol soap's germ-fighting image by showing a soap that was similar to it in colour and size, RB complained about HUL airing the advertisement.

Dettol vs Lifebuoy Handwash

In a triumphant move calculated to make Lifebuoy synonymous with washing hands, HUL's Lifebuoy grabbed the 'official sponsor' status for Global Handwashing Day. The day was 15 October 2009, and for months leading up to the event HUL ran campaigns across media to raise awareness about the benefits of handwashing.

Arch-rival Dettol, plotted a squeaky-clean victory. It ran a campaign that simply told people, 'Germs are everywhere, every day...' and asked them, therefore, to 'make every day a handwash day.' Even as HUL worked on building awareness about a special day celebrating handwashing, Dettol cashed in on the opportunity and claimed the platform for itself. The campaign definitely made its presence felt, quite hijacking rival efforts.

Cadbury's Perk vs Nestlé Munch

In 2016, India consumed 228,000 tonnes worth of chocolate with the Indian chocolate market posting a 13 per cent growth in sales.[5]

However, even though overall chocolate consumption has been steadily increasing in India, it is still not as widespread as it could be. *Mithai* can, and does, compete with chocolate for our sweet tooth, but to those inclined towards chocolate, Cadbury India Ltd (today Mondelez India Foods Private Limited), has been the name they know best.

---

[5] 'India Among World's Fastest Growing Chocolate Markets: Research', *Times of India*, 30 April 2017

Consumers have also traditionally been found willing to try small, differentiated offerings. That is exactly the space where chocolate-wrapped wafers, Cadbury Perk and Nestlé Munch, have always competed in.

In 2013, Munch made the cricketer Virat Kohli its brand ambassador. This move made it imperative for Perk to show their strength. With the existing battle lines becoming wafer-thin, a Perk ad took a punch at Munch.

The Perk ad told Sonu, Monu *tey Pappa di* story.

It revolved around a letter written by Monu, outlining how he had decided to leave home because his dad had discriminated against him. His dad had given Monu a chocolate that was only 11.5 gram – and what was worse, it had only three wafers! (The chocolate being referred to was clearly a Munch.) As for the heavyweight Perk, weighing 17 gram, with not three but *four* wafers – it had been given to Sonu. In his letter Monu wrote that he was extremely hurt by this favouritism where he had been given the obviously inferior chocolate. The ad ended with the voiceover, 'The new twin bar of Cadbury Perk Glucose – extra wafer, extra chocolate, extra *pyaar*.'

It marked the beginning of a bar brawl.

Nestlé retaliated quickly with a spoof of the Perk ad. It began with a dad going to awaken his son, Sonu, for school, and seeing a letter. The letter accused the father of loving Monu more and giving him the crunchier, more delicious Munch. While poor Sonu was given the heavier, not-as-good chocolate (quite obviously a Perk). After all, 'Chocolate *hum* taste *ke liye khate hai,* weight *ke liye nahin,*' the dad said. He also suggested using 'the heavy chocolate as a paperweight', and asked, 'Before eating a *parantha*, do you ask mom about its weight?' The ad ended with a voiceover, 'Crunchiest ever, tastiest ever – Nestlé Munch.'

Munch used humour to divert attention from 'sizeable' issues. There was no doubt about it – it was a smart, aggressive reply to the Perk ad. And a much-needed reply at that, because social networking dynamics make it imperative that brands are responsive, visible and quick. Twitter and Facebook had a good laugh over the Perk vs Munch war. Tweets chuckled over how you 'should not throw your weight around because Munch can pack a punch!' Some 'perked' up to see the chocolate wafer ad war while others said they wanted to 'weight and watch'. Meanwhile, many voted for the 'punchy comeback from Munch'.

But the ultimate winner of the war was the chocolate wafer category itself, because, while the hugely entertaining ads protected the brands, they also caught the attention of consumers, some of whom, no doubt, would have gone out and bought themselves one or the other brand of delicious chocolate wafers.

Horlicks vs Complan

In 2008, Horlicks was a ₹1,000 crore brand in a ₹1,800 crore market, which was growing at 20 per cent annually.[6] For

[6] Bhushan, Ratna and Paramita Chatterjee, 'Horlicks, Complan Slug It Out Over Price Points', *Economic Times*, 23 December 2008

GlaxoSmithKline (GSK) Consumer HealthCare, this was a happy place as Horlicks had a 55 per cent share in the health food and drinks category. GSK's other brand, Boost, had a 14 per cent market share and was just a bit ahead of Heinz's Complan.

Over the years, various brands in the category had aggressively introduced variants to accommodate buyers' preferences while broadening the consumer base. Each time, each of the brands had eyed the competition as it flaunted its assets and tried to do better.

When GSK and Heinz eventually went on the warpath, it was about not one but a few communication pieces. The main points these hinged on were growth and quality – and, of course, the quantity of nutrients in each drink.

Horlicks – probably thinking there couldn't be too much of a good thing – decided to add to its appeal by appropriating Complan's claims. It released a television commercial involving both the brands in question – Complan and Horlicks. The film opened on two kids and their mothers, thus bringing all the decision-makers into the frame. The setup makes it clear that the mothers have been shopping and are now indulging in brand one-upmanship. Complan had for long built its brand on the selling point that it contained '23 vital nutrients'. In the ad, the Horlicks kid tells the Complan boy that not only is his Horlicks as strong on nutrition, it also makes him taller, stronger and sharper. 'It's proven,' he says. What's more, he asks his mother and confirms that his drink, Horlicks, is priced lower than its competitor by over ₹40.

The ad ends with a shot of the pack and a line reiterating the brands promise of 'taller, stronger, sharper'.

In the Complan commercial that followed, the Horlicks-Mummy was seen asking the Complan-Mummy how her son was so tall and strong. Now, as we all know, this is the question that worries mothers across the country. So the Complan mother helpfully rattled off the benefits of drinking Complan. Then came the 'cheap' shot. She asked the other mother whether she has ever read the label on a Horlicks bottle and went on to explain how Horlicks was made of cheap ingredients. This logically implied lesser nourishment and inferior protein content. The ad ended with a voiceover praising Complan.

Both sides decided to stick to their claims and challenge the other's and for better or for worse, matters landed in court.

Good Day vs UNIBIC Cookies

You gotta risk it to get the biscuit. But it's not all that easy because the *biskut* market in India is not all sweet. While the consumer has always been willing to flirt with different brands, Britannia Industries Limited and Sunfeast Biscuits (an ITC brand) have proved to be formidable opponents for anyone trying to creep in.

In 2016, Good Day from Britannia had a 9 per cent share in the ₹25,000-crore domestic biscuit market.[7] Established

---

[7] Sarkar, John, 'Biscuits Losing Space in Cookie Jar', *Times of India*, 10 June 2016

in 1892, apparently with a meagre capital of ₹295, Britannia is well-established in India today, manufacturing and supplying biscuits (including iconic brands such as Bourbon, Tiger, Little Hearts and Good Day), rusks, cakes and bread, apart from sundry dairy products.

Among its biscuit brands, Good Day has been a registered trademark of Britannia since 1986. As a brand name it has lent itself easily to Britannia, sunnily telling consumers to 'Have a good day'.

So it must have been a bad day in 2007, when Britannia woke up to a print ad that said, 'Why have a good day when you can have a great day!' The visual showed cookies dipped in the ingredients from which they were made. The cookies and the ad had been released by UNIBIC India (the Indian arm of UNIBIC Cookies, Australia). To drive home the good-versus-great point, the ad went on to urge consumers to not settle for anything less than great. It also claimed that UNIBIC Cookies were made from the finest ingredients and were far better than 'any other mere biscuit'. The sign-off concluded with, 'UNIBIC Cookies. You deserve a great day!' Meanwhile, the company released a television commercial that also contained targeted statements like 'Forget the good'.

The words 'Good Day' are actually a registered property of Britannia. If you look closely at packs of the biscuits you will find a tiny R (the mandatory 'registered' mark) next to the words. This means they cannot be used to advertise any other business, product or service, and any usage that violates or exploits the property is liable for legal action.

So when UNIBIC advertised their cookies using these words, Britannia could (and did) cry foul in the courts.

It turns out that a simple phrase like, 'Good Day' can have a crushing effect.

Eveready vs Havells

The joke goes that there can't be an LED Beauty Contest because the winner would then be Mis-LED. Be that as it may, there can be a Brightest LED Bulb Contest and one player can accuse another of mis-LE(a) D-ing the consumer.

The Indian LED (or Light Emitting Diode) industry's *kismet* has been acquiring quite a beauteous *chamak*. LED bulbs are swiftly replacing traditional bulbs in popularity. In 2016, India was said to be consuming 12 per cent of all LED lighting systems sold in the world. The government of India, too, has declared its intention to switch to LED systems for all lighting in public spaces.[8] With the spread of knowledge about the benefits of sustainable energy, the LED segment is all set to leap forward, the plans of individual manufacturers of the product extending beyond the production of LED bulbs to streetlights, accent lights and everything in between, and since the future is looking

[8] Dutta, Sanjay, 'India Headed For Top Slot in Global LED Bulb Market', *Times of India*, 21 April 2016

so bright it is quite logical for lighting brands to get into street(light)-fights.

One of the companies in this space, Eveready Industries India Ltd, traditionally a manufacturer of batteries and flashlights, has stepped into the LED lights space in recent years. It is deeply focused on the lighting segment of its business, which it expects will grow at a rapid rate.

It was an Eveready ad featuring the Bollywood star Akshay Kumar that sparked off the LED battle. The ad made everyone sit up because it had a chart comparing its LED bulbs with LED bulbs from Halonix, Philips, Havells, Syska, Bajaj and Surya. The main points of scrutiny were lumens (a measure of the brightness of light emitted per second from a luminous device), lumens per watt and price. The ad cautioned consumers to check the lumens as well as the price of an LED bulb before buying it. Their message was clear as daylight: Eveready gives the brightest light at a competitive price.

One of the company's competitors, Havells, took Eveready to court, saying that the ad was aimed at misleading consumers and that lumens were not the only parameter to be considered while determining the quality of an LED bulb. As a measure of the amount of visible light from a source, lumens only measure brightness. What about power, which is an equally important consideration? And what about the life of the product?

Eveready contended that it had compared the common features mentioned in the packaging of various brands and

Havells' appeal was dismissed. And it maintained that lumens are the most important aspect of a bulb because its primary function is to give light.

In the end, a brand's wit counts for great memorability. Wars need not leave a bitter taste in anyone's mouth, especially if you are talking chocolate. As Cadbury's told us '*Meetha hai khana, aaj pehli tareekh hai!*' Not to be left behind, Nestlé offered us their *meetha*, saying '*Khao bina tareekh ke!*'

Sometimes, though, a third party carries away the chocolate. Quite like that proverbial helpful monkey who eats up the entire bar even as his two friends squabble with each other over their shares. There was a time when Kingfisher, the king of good times, seemed to be having such a rollicking time in the aviation business that it sent its rival, Jet Airways, into a panic. Jet decided to get into a rebranding exercise showcasing its customer friendliness and service. As a part of this, Jet Airways put up a hoarding that read, 'We've changed'. Kingfisher Airlines placed a billboard right above Jet's hoarding saying, 'We made them change!'. As clever and cheeky as that was, in this instance nobody had counted on GoAir stealing the show. Placing a hoarding even above the one belonging to Kingfisher, GoAir announced, 'We've not changed. We are still the smartest way to fly.'

Similarly, even as Pepsi and Coke spent obscene amounts of money slugging it out in the marketplace, Indian consumers watched the battle while swigging their favourite cola, Thums Up. Thums Up was the brand Coca-Cola bought when it entered India. It was also the drink people meanly wondered about being re-named *Thooke*. Not only did it prove too popular to be spat out, today it even has a mountain in its honour. The Thums Up peak, commonly called that because of its similarity to the logo, is in the Manmad Hills in Nasik, Maharashtra, and is a popular sighting from trains that pass by.

Brand-Mahabharats may start with companies making mountains out of molehills, but how many brands actually have a mountain to their name?

Lingo Dance, Lingo Dance

DESI AD TALK

If there's one thing that binds all kinds of people across the country, it's bad language. Why, for a while there, the entire nation was singing a movie song that went '*Bhaag bhaagDKBoseDKBoseDKBoseDKBoseDKBoseDK*'. So at least as far as swear words are concerned, the nation has definitely started attaining unity in diversity.

Experts point out that this is because some local words have that indefinable something, that overarching appeal, which makes them rise above mere regional boundaries. Which is why '*Behen**od*, where've you been, *maadar**od!*' has become an affectionate form of greeting across many states.

If abuses are a definitive way of communicating, so is slang – and although they are 'local' by nature, they, too, can rise above borders. In 2011, the slangy, Tamglish lyrics of the song 'Why This Kolaveri Di' went viral on social networking sites – not just among people from Tamil Nadu but across the country. A cover version of the song even featured in a 2015 Coca-Cola ad in far-off Turkey (while in 2014, 'Bhaag DK Bose' too inspired the data product from MTS, MBlaze Ultra, to come up with a music video on 'Browse, browse DK Bose').

Of course, advertising has often been quick to pick up on people-speak and utilized it to address markets. It has creatively used language, local pronunciation and accents, colloquialisms and sometimes even nonsense to come up with linguistic curiosities and some remarkable pieces of communication.

But it was not always so. In the beginning, many of the mainstream ads had styling and language that was conventional. Bengali, Tamil or Malayalam were distinct languages and used as such. Hindi was chaste and English was gentlemanly and the two did not meet, let alone produce offspring.

By the 1980s, though, a generation that had been introduced to English by chanting 'Ding-dong bell, pussy's in the well...' was inexplicably crooning, '*Dingg-dong, O bebby sing-a-song*! *Aaj ki sham ka*...'

This was gold. And it was unmistakably mined-in-India. Hinglish – that love-child of English and Hindi – became the trendsetter but there were several other versions – there was Bonglish, Tamglish and well, Malish. The speakers were often called all kinds of names – pidgin, *khichdi* or ruder stuff which loosely translated to 'O bastard son of English'.

But it was clear that the desi lingo was here to stay. Advertising, always eager to be part of the latest trends, embraced the lingo, the pronunciations, the slangs and the local embellishments. And for a few decades now, all these things have been showing up more and more – in quirky jingles and even in sign-offs for brands.

When the old order changeth, it does not do so too slowly-slowly, you know. So, unsurprisingly, many of these ad phrases and expressions have fast become part of popular culture.

Binnie's Chips

Remember a grammatically-challenged potato chips' brand saying '...Binnie's *maangta*'?

When the 1990s began, the Binnie's potato chips television commercial and jingle were on top of everyone's mind:

Naya naya ye chips Binnie's,
Iski har baat nayi.
Chips hai ye bahut pyaara, tasty aur karara,
Iseeliye toh ye meri jaan hai, jaan hai, jaan hai!
Humko yeh nahin maangta,
Humko woh nahin maangta,
Humko aur koi chips nahin maangta.
Toh kya maangta?
Humko Binnie's maangta!
Binnie's, Binnie's!

Refreshingly different and with *tapori*-cool attitude, the film became quite a milestone in advertising and was a huge success. The jingle was hummable and catchy and soon everyone was adding *maangta* to their lexicon.

By 1990, Jagatjit Industries Limited, which owned the Binnie's brand, got a taste of big success in the north and launched in Mumbai, trying to battle it out with the unorganized sector. At the time, the potato-chips industry in India was worth ₹400 crore and was growing at an incredible rate of 30 per cent annually. Everyone wanted a share. But branded chips comprised only 10 per cent of the market and the rest of the competition was from the local *mithaiwala*.[1]

Then Pepsi entered the fray with its own brand of potato chips and advertising muscle. Jagatjit Industries Limited took on the challenge in various ways. It tried offering a free glass with two packs of Binnie's Chips. It even introduced rippled potato chips and increased the number of flavours available. But the sales, if they did go up, did not do so for long.

Today, nobody *maangta* Binnie's, but the jingle remains iconic in making *desi*-speak part of the mainstream.

Channel V

It was in the 1990s that cable TV arrived in the country, and along with it came eagerly anticipated music channels with *angrezi gaane*. Before that, listening to Western music was a fix you mostly got in measured, late-night portions on Doordarshan or AIR.

Indian English saw a turning-point of sorts with the coming of cable TV. In 1994, Channel V started a new campaign which spoofed the way we Indians speak English. It was funny, it was insightful, and it gave us identities we liked flaunting.

It starred Quick Gun Murugan, a *sambar*-loving Southie cowboy. He started out by asking for 'one whisky,

[1] Das Gupta, Surajeet, 'A Crackling Challenge', *India Today*, 15 April 1990

one *masala dosa'*. When he challenged the bad guy he said, 'If you've drunk your mother's milk, come to the fields, *wokay*?' And he told a woman, 'The room in my heart is already rented.'

No *mai ka laal* was quite like Quick Gun Murugan. Soon the theatrical character gained a large following – with fans spouting the thickly accented gems that studded his dialogue: classics like 'Mind it', 'We are like this only' and 'What to do'.

Today, Quick Gun Murugun is still such a cult figure that Shah Rukh Khan even did a sequence inspired by him in the movie *Om Shanti Om*.

Channel V's brand of desi English resonated instantly with the youth, giving their lingo a platform. Street English – looked down upon by purists – became acceptable, even cool, on campuses and hangouts. Channel V had provided the country with a mirror that showed its own quirky reflection.

The campaign worked brilliantly. It cleverly took care of two angles – it made the brand feel more 'Indian' while taking care of our fondness for all things Western.

The channel's penetration of the Indian market saw a six-time jump by 1996. When the eagerly-awaited MTV came in, it quickly learned its lesson from its predecessor. Although it was a cosmopolitan brand if ever there was one, MTV too adopted *desi* trappings.

Soon enough, we found all kinds of products and ads reaching out to us by cultivating a mixed avatar. Which pleased us because many of us had already been spicing up our daily conversations with unorthodox words.

And that's how V had tasted *wictory*, India-style. We had always found English a *phunny* language and now we were going to make an awesome *falooda* out of it.

Domino's Pizza

What is called *pijha* in Maharashtra and *pijja* in UP will probably not be recognized in Italy.

To the non-Indian, Domino's offerings in India would be curious to say the least. Chicken tikka pizzas beckon enticingly alongside thin crust margheritas – a happy result of the company's familiarity with the consumer.

When Domino's launched in India with an outlet in Delhi, its biggest rival was Pizza Hut, which had entered the country earlier. They both faced similar problems in dealing with the Indian mindset. Pizza was not really a snack but was not quite a meal either, especially to the Indians used to roti-*dal-chawal*.

What Domino's needed was a platform that could tie in both the snack and the meal to eating a pizza, customized for the Indian palate. And what better way to do it than by focusing on 'hunger'?

For a consumer-conscious quick-service restaurant brand, Indianizing the menu led to the logical next step – Indianizing the communication.

So in 2000, within a few years of setting up in India, Dominos came up with a campaign centred around 'Hungry *kya*?' The language was in keeping with the Indian pizzas on the menu. 'Hungry *kya*' lent itself as a phrase to many kinds of hunger, not all of them for food. The situations were comical and the line, with its easy appeal, caught on.

In one of these ads, you had a man barely able to control his hand as it dialled for a cheese-burst pizza from Domino's. In another, a *thakur*, about to be attacked by a certain Dacoit Singh, enticed the bad guys with pizza (smartly procured at a very affordable special price) before getting them arrested.

'Hungry *kya*' reiterated that pizza could easily switch from being a snack to being a meal in itself. While this was a campaign to drive home the connection between hunger and Domino's home delivery, it also delivered on memorability.

Alongside the ads, Domino's employed several smart strategies to get their pizzas moving. This included the usuals – special offer coupons as well as phone calls to frequent customers. The promise of a sizzling-hot home delivery within thirty minutes made ordering from them even more enticing. Many found themselves hooked after a few trials. By 2014, Domino's was the largest pizza brand in the country and India had become one of its largest markets.

The corporate name of Domino's Pizza India Ltd has since changed to Jubilant FoodWorks Ltd (JFL) and today it boasts of a massive network of outlets.

Today, from Raipur to Ranchi, eating a pizza is no longer an encounter with a strange food item. In fact, it has become somewhat of a norm for a treat, or food for a gathering or, more recently, for no reason at all.

A 2017 commercial even showed a family ordering a pizza just like that, because why wait for an occasion? Order '*Jab dil boley*,' the brand tells you.

By then one thing is clear: the heart may not be speaking *shuddh* Italian, but however you said it, *peeja* Hindustani is here to stay.

Tata Sky

Imagine a jungle teeming with wild ethnic persons shaking their booty. Now picture a moping man in a castle who sings a sad song about love and betrayal. Camera takes in The Wild Things, then focusses on Mopey, then The Wild Things, then Mopey again...the tension builds. What is going to happen?

Are the tribal folk going to comfort Mopey? Are they going to kidnap him? Are they going to kill him? *Arrey, arrey*...they are going to...

...prance around singing – *Jingalala, hurr, hurrr*!

?!!??

Really.

Inexplicably in the old Bollywood flick, *Shalimar*, people with flaming tiki-torches sang *Jingalala, jingalala, hurr, hurr* on loop while *Garam Dharam*(endra) moped prettily.

But c'mon, it was Bollywood. Everyone accepted it had odd moments.

But a few decades later, when DTH service provider, Tata Sky began yelling *jingalala* at its audience, people did a double take. There were no indigenous people in body-baring regalia in the Tata Sky ads. So no native language excuse.

Yet, there was Tata Sky saying in impeccable nonsenshinglish, '*Isko laga daala toh* life *jingalala*.'

How did Tata Sky arrive at this expression?

The story goes back to the early 2000s when Direct To Home (DTH) had just about begun making the rounds as a service. It was perceived to be a substitute for poor or no cable connectivity. Even when it began gaining mild acceptance, it was thought to be a premium product and everyone believed that DTH would remain a niche business. However, advanced technology provided better viewing quality and later, better programming and content, DTH slowly began winning the consumer over. It began to be seen as a nice-to-have service, especially in urban areas.[2]

As demand grew, Tata Sky became a fast-growing direct-to-home service provider.

Brand communication played a role in this growth. Most communication in the category had been feature-led – full of jargon and technological chest-thumping. Tata Sky television commercials were noticeable because they were informal and showcased the brand in

[2] Das Gupta, Surajeet, '10 Years of DTH in India', *Business Standard*, 1 January 2014

a simple way. After all, why intimidate folks by saying the 'tech' word when you could endearingly refer to it all as *jingalala*?

This '*Isko laga daala toh* life *jingalala*' line had charm (in a weird way) and it had breadth. It could be used to communicate many different things.

In its communication, Tata Sky had, at various times, roped in Hrithik Roshan, Kirron Kher and Paresh Rawal for standalone campaigns or ads.

By 2008, Bharti Airtel had launched Airtel Digital TV and Dish TV, from the Essel Group, had got Shah Rukh Khan to tell people 'Wish *karo*, Dish *karo*'. Tata Sky decided it was time to make Aamir Khan its brand ambassador and use him strategically to take the brand forward.

Since Tata Sky was a joint venture between Tata Sons and Sky (a Rupert Murdoch company), one of its films set out to establish exactly this. It featured Aamir Khan in a double role as a single character.

Well, not really single, because he was actually a couple – half of him dressed as a man, half as a woman, both halves engaged in a full-on argument. The female half was convinced about getting Sky with its 'foreign', world-class technology, while the male half wanted Tata with all that the name stood for.

But there was no argument really, as the half-and-half Aamir pointed out. Because Tata and Sky were joined/married already – giving you Tata Sky – with its great technology, computer-like features and picture quality. And of course, *jo* family *dekhe* TV Tata Sky *ke saath*, *wo humesha rahe saath saath*. Cue to living happily ever after because '*Isko laga dala toh* life *jingalala*.'

In another ad, Aamir Khan was shown as the guy who wanted to watch cricket but his wife was watching TV. She then told him both were possible with Tata Sky. You could record one programme while watching another. '*Isko laga dala toh* life *aur bhi jingalala*,' the voiceover told you.

Fast forward to 2016, when the line still had swag. Tata Sky had roped in Amitabh Bachchan (in no less than seven puppet-inspired roles) to narrate, rapper-style, the story of the Thakur clan – how individual family member needs could be met by subscribing to Tata Sky – the best DTH connection for a varied range of entertainment. *Isko laga daala toh* family *jingalala*, you were told by a bohemian-looking Bachchan.

So with time, *jingalala* had come to mean many things – choice, convenience, control. Apart from various recording-related features, Tata Sky released mobile streaming apps and interactive services for individual family members – from education to cooking, temple-darshans to sports. All this at attractive price bundles and discounts. The ads clearly communicated that life and TV viewing could be much more *jingalala* with Tata Sky.

The phrase had currency, it had longevity and it had Presence. Like it or not, you could not ignore *jingalala*, especially when everyone around you was mouthing it either as a joke or as a throwaway line. (Some wits even latched on to the *isko laga dala* part and asked if *isko* referred to a condom.)

In the long run, it turned out that *jingalala* was 'open to interpretation'. And so, even though the DTH-consuming audience may have debated the phrase, they found it rolled off the tongue quite easily. As it turned out, Tata Sky became one of the top DTH players in the country.

So just like the cryptic tribals had chorused in the Bollywood *jingalala* song, for Tata Sky things worked out pretty much '*Hurrr, Hurrr*!'

Close Up

The Indian toothpaste industry is dazzling at the very least. Just thinking of the *battissee*, or the set of 32 teeth, within each mouth of our teeming millions can make a marketer's calculator crash and his heart soar.

Yet, it takes many things to get people to put their money where their mouths are. Some brands hang on only by the skin of their teeth. The reason is that the market is ruled by a number of considerations – price and emotional benefit being just some of the stand-out factors. Plus, many Indians, especially in rural areas, swear by their daily brush with a *neem* stick, and you cannot wish away the significance of toothpowder as well. Habit and value-consciousness are behind the use of these products and brands.

Value-consciousness also pulls in customers for Babool and Promise while Patanjali's Dant Kanti, Meswak and Himalaya Dental Cream promise traditional therapy in addition to being reasonably priced.

So companies like Colgate Palmolive, HUL and P&G instead focus on protection in their major campaigns, and of course, on the one-upping role your toothsome-ness plays when you want to win friends and influence people.

In 1975, Hindustan Lever (now HUL) launched Close Up with quite a few firsts to its name. It was the first gel toothpaste in India, it was also the first to primarily target the youth. In the 1980s, it introduced the breath self-check. The ads encouraged you to breathe 'haaaaaa' on to your palm to ensure your mouth wasn't all *hawww* and malodorous.

It was a different product from the other toothpastes in the market, so its advertising also focused on all things different. But by 2004, the difference was not being perceived in terms of sales. So HUL added vitamin and fluoride to the mix, trying to up the perception of oral care along with fresh breath. Variants like 'Oxy Fresh', 'Eucalyptus Blue' and 'Lemon' were launched. But these variants did not bring in the returns that the huge media spends demanded. The problem was that Close Up had recall as a sensory brand. Variants with health attributes were just not as convincing.

So, later in 2004, came one of the most-remembered toothpaste campaigns ever – the very Hinglish '*Kya aap* Close Up *karte hain*?'

The ad starred characters from a world that the generation the brand was targeting found retro – girls with thickly lined eyes and broad hairbands, boys with colourful shirts and pop-out collars. Added to this were polka dots, bright colours and singing – the old-school nasal singing style that cut through the incessant TV commercial jingle jungle. It was the singing style from the days of Saigal and Suraiyya, which everyone loved spoofing at the time.

The ad showed a girl walking down a street when a well-coiffed guy blew her a kiss. So bad was his breath that she was repulsed, only to fall, right away, for the charms of another guy who breathed fresh clouds from his mouth.

The visuals were simplistic and retro. The protagonist was an Amol-Palekar-from-*Golmaal* type who got the gorgeous girl by the simple act of blowing her a kiss. Comic-book style, it reached her loaded with *taazgi*. The dude with the slick hair was clearly no match for the Close-Up guy.

The catchy jingle was easy to sing. And fun too. You just pinched your nostrils and went:

Kya aap Close Up karte hain?
Ya duniya se darte hain?
Aur penalty bharte hain?
Aap Close Up kyon nahin karte hain?

The brand promised youthful audiences uninhibited *kaanfidence* in social situations with the overriding association of the brand with fresh breath. Basically, you could get up close and personal with confidence.

The nasal voice was disruptive and easy to imitate; the jingle was extremely hummable and catchy. And the Hinglish, retro treatment – though familiar – was new for the category.

Coming as it did in a space where you normally saw cute kids being taught how to brush to get rid of all the *keetanoo* on their teeth, the execution was completely fresh. It paved the way for many 'me-too' ads, videos and radio spots which showcased the ad's characteristic nasal voice.

It stuck with everyone who saw it and even today, it is a much-recalled spot about how that guy (*aye-haye*) got fresh with (*woohoo*), that girl.

In the end, what matters is connecting with your consumer. And as many Indian brands have found out, a good way to do it is with desi-speak. Since the 1990s, this is one pan-Indian relationship that has never looked back. As McDonald's put it, 'We are loving it!'

Or is it making your '*Bheja fry*? 7 Up try'.

Pepsi had its '*Youngistaan meri jaan*!' and it also had '*Yeh dil maange* more!' with regional variations like the Tamglish, '*Ullam kekku thae* more.'

And more is still to come. To rephrase an old saying, '*Aagey, aagey dekho*, then what happened!'

Yes, yes. We are seeing only.

Badalne Ki Aag

AGENTS OF CHANGE

Change can be ushered-in in interesting ways. The United Nations once announced that Wonder Woman – you know, the superheroine with the unattainable figure, Playboy Bunny looks, star-spangled *choli-blouse* and thigh-baring bottomwear, would be the UN honorary ambassador for (hold your breath) gender empowerment. Her role was to be backed by DC Entertainment and Warner Bros, who were behind the Wonder Woman sagas. Though controversial, this wasn't the first time that the UN had partnered with a fictional or commercialized character, as Winnie the Pooh and Tinkerbell can testify. And logical or not, such appointments definitely signified a different approach to complex issues.

Closer home, too, organizations often think up new ways of doing things. They can be seen trying to bring about change with a little help from mascots. Or interacting with seemingly unreachable audiences by thinking out of the box.

Look at the example of the cartoon cutie with blue hair who became the face of the Amul milk-marketing revolution. Take the sometimes sombre, sometimes super-starry campaign against polio. Look at that man who got the masses to shampoo their hair by packaging his product in affordable little sachets. Or the company that pushed its detergent in media-dark areas by providing entertainment on the ubiquitous cellphone.

Whether the change-making is in the way of thinking, or in doing; whether it involves community participation, awareness, greater outreach or rural marketing – advertising can play a key role. There are many, many incredible examples of marketing and communication catalyzing change. And, oftentimes, taking care of profitability too.

Amul

It is not often that a dairy farmer imagines his produce being sold by a girl without a nose. But just such a little girl with blue hair and a polka-dotted frock has been the 'pun-dit' in Amul milk products' ads for over fifty years now.

Way back in 1946, when Tribhuvandas Patel started a cooperative in Kaira, it was because he believed that development begins at the grass roots. The aim was to empower the farmers themselves.

So the cooperative put the milk collectors around the village of Anand in Gujarat in control of the procurement, processing and marketing of milk. Fresh milk was collected at a place easily accessible to the milk producers. It then went to the Village Dairy Cooperative, the District Milk Cooperative Union and the State Cooperative Milk Marketing Federation before ending up at the home of the consumer.

It was a brand new way of doing things. Guided by visionaries like Dr Verghese Kurien, the Gujarat Cooperative Milk Marketing Federation became a professionally-managed system which eliminated middlemen. It also propelled the village of Anand into becoming the milk capital of India. As the Amul girl later quipped about Kurien, he 'brought Anand to millions of farmers'.

Where there is milk, can butter be far behind? For a certain generation, their bread and butter depends on one thing – Amul. They grew up on Amul butter, and no other can ever taste quite the same. But interestingly enough, the taste of Amul butter may actually have come about as a backlash against a brand called Polson.

In 1910, Pestonji, the owner of Polson's Coffee in Mumbai, was looking around for business opportunities. He decided on starting a dairy business in Kaira in Gujarat, with the aim of supplying to the British Army. Not only did this help close a gap in the army's supply chain, Polson's soon became a name synonymous with butter and Pestonji became the guy with a stranglehold on the market.

In his autobiography, *I Too Had a Dream*, Dr Kurien recounted how Polson always made butter from stale cream. Sometimes these cans of cream would be kept for as long as ten days without refrigeration. Polson's was not bothered since they had found a way to remove bad odours in the manufacturing process but Amul was determined to make their butter only from fresh cream. The idea was to take the cream from the milk and make butter out of it, all in the same day.

The butter bombed in the market. People felt it tasted flat and flavourless. The sour cream Polson's used, along with heavy salting to help preserve the butter, had given

Polson's a distinctive taste which customers had grown accustomed to and didn't want changed!

Amul had to come up with a solution. It found that adding a chemical additive called diacetyl brought about the 'required' butter taste that the consumers were so used to. So did increasing the salt content. Add some yellow to colour the white buffalo-milk butter and soon Amul's butter was doing much better than Polson's. It ultimately went on to decimate the latter, and Polson lovers were replaced by a generation that grew up eating, and loving, Amul butter. Which is why the salty Polson taste that Amul recreated is still favoured, long after the company that created it is gone.

Apart from the taste, Amul took on Polson in other ways. One story goes, early in the morning, long before the Polson butter supply arrived, Amul salesmen would arrive at popular eateries in Mumbai – wherever they thought the working population would step in for breakfast – and distribute small packs of Amul butter, effectively cutting off the need for Polson.

Dr Kurien realized early on that to hold its own in the market, Amul would need to advertise. In 1966, the tagline was 'Purely the best', and it needed a change.

The agency – daCunha Communications – was told that Amul butter had to be promoted as butter 'processed from the purest milk under the most hygienic conditions by a dairy cooperative in Gujarat'.

Inspiring stuff...it was not.

It was snoozeworthy and that's what the campaign may have been too but for Sylvester daCunha, the then manager of the agency. DaCunha thought what might work was something different, something like 'Utterly, butterly Amul'.

'Utterly mad,' Dr Kurien reportedly reacted. But in what has always been the marketing style for Amul, he also trusted that the experts knew what they were doing. He told the agency that if it believed the line would work, they should go ahead with it.

Dr Kurien also gave a thumbs-up to a little person drawn by Eustace Fernandes at the agency. This was the Amul butter girl, created to compete with the chubby Polson's girl. Wanting to make something different, Fernandes did away with the nose and used five colours to create this character – black outlines, an orange face, blue hair, a red polka- dotted dress and a green tag line.

She debuted on lamp post boards in Mumbai drawing smiles, and soon, an outdoor campaign was built around the character. There she was, piously kneeling, praying for her 'daily bread with Amul butter', with one eye on an Amul butter pack. 'Thoroughbread,' went the line above the picture of her riding a racehorse.

After an initial series of much-noticed outdoor communication and ads, daCunha decided that the creative pieces needed a concept that would bind them together and boost the brand communication.

In 1969, the Hare Rama, Hare Krishna movement was gaining momentum. When the Amul line said, 'Hurry

Amul, Hurry Hurry', people loved it for its topicality, and that went on to become the theme.

With a cheeky and cheerful flavour, the ads made an entertainment-hungry India chuckle. Over the years, people began looking forward to Amul's evocative humour on all things newsworthy.

The need was felt for a quick response to news-making events. So Dr Kurien waived the week-long approval process that hoarding designs were put through and gave the agency a free hand. That leap of faith is still paying off. When M.F. Husain kept painting a Bollywood star, the Amul girl commented on his 'heroine addiction'. '*Kha na*, Hazare,' she cajoled a fasting Anna Hazare, holding out buttered bread. And the butter was 'Item No.1' as the Amul girl moved to 'Sheila *ki makhani*'.

Contemporaneity has always been Amul's strength. With time, the brand's ads have become more and more customized, depending on their relevance for the media platform used and the geographical area being targeted. Even the role of the Amul girl is different on each platform.

In the outdoor medium, she is a social observer – the strategy being to comment on India. But the strategy for television is to sell a range of products which makes her role more hard-working. And how could the Amul girl miss out on social networking? In the last few years, the brand has increased its digital spends with emphasis on using Facebook and Twitter as platforms for its topical outdoor creatives.

For most of us, Amul butter and the moppet are inseparable from our first memories about butter itself. That is part of the legacy of Dr Kurien, who the Amul girl credits with 'making India a butter place'.

In FY 2016–17, Amul's sales figures were over ₹27,085 crore in FY 2015–16.[1] Competition is heating up though. There is butter from Mother Dairy, Britannia, Vijaya and Kwality, to name just a few. And since people look for lower-salt content products now, is it possible that some consumers may switch loyalty?

No matter how the industry may change, the little girl in the polka-dotted dress remains the 'toast' (buttered, of course) of one of the greatest movements of Independent India.

In this case, a bit of butter did make everything better.

Lijjat Papad

Few companies can say that a buck-toothed rabbit helped them along on their road to success. But then, Lijjat Papad is not like most companies. For instance, how many companies start out with a capital of ₹80 collected from a few housewives?

In 1959, there was little by way of heat-and-eat products in the market. Jaswantiben Popat and her six friends, who lived in a housing colony in Girgaum, Mumbai, did

[1] 'Amul Turnover Grows 18% to Rs 27,085 Crore in 2016–17', *Business Standard*, 1 April 2017

not know much about production, marketing or, for that matter, advertising. What they did know was how to make papad. And so they scraped together ₹80 to buy supplies, talked to a nearby grocer and set up production on a terrace.

The first batch they made consisted only four or five packs of papad. In a few months' time, however, the demand skyrocketed. The product was flying off the shelves like, well, hot *papadums*.

Soon it became a very viable community effort. To make money, more and more women began to help out and, more quickly than anyone could have imagined, there were over a hundred workers. More hands meant more output, and more profits.

But the increase in demand led to space becoming an issue and, therefore, called for somewhat unconventional measures. The women were now given the ingredients to take home where they could work on making the papad exactly as was expected. They came back the next day with the packs of papad that they had rolled out and dried in their homes. Their contribution was taken stock of, accounted for, packaged and sold.

So while self-sufficiency was key, interdependence within the outfit was high. As the years progressed, Lijjat even hired buses that transported the women to and from their homes, leading to more efficient and streamlined working processes.

Word about the papad spread and the production capacity of this dynamic cooperative kept increasing. By 1966, Lijjat was registered as a society.

An important aspect of Lijjat's success was its focus on quality control, which was stringent. The ingredients and techniques used were all standardized. Only the pieces that passed muster made it into the market. The others were given away locally.

Then there was the communication. You may not agree with the choice of a giant *khargosh* singing *karram-kurram*, but the image of him with papad in hand, accompanied by the little boy, Babla, also seen with papad, had unquestionable brand recall. And Lijjat has kept this association alive across decades.

Ramdas Padhye, a ventriloquist, created the iconic rabbit mascot in 1979 for a Lijjat brand film. The *karram-kurram* and the he-he-he sounds in the jingle were his contributions too, which made the Lijjat rabbit came alive for a whole generation in the 1980s in the form of television commercials. He sang out '*karram-kurram*' from the TV screen as he and his pals gobbled Lijjat papad.[2]

'*Shadi utsav ya tyohaar*, Lijjat papad *ho har baar, karram-kurram, kurram-karram, mazedaar lazzatdaar saat swaad mein* Lijjat Lijjat papad...'

Or 'Chai coffee *ke sang khaiye, karram-kurram, mehmanon ko khush karjaye, kurram-karram, mazedaar lazzatdaar saat swaad mein* Lijjat Lijjat papad!'

---

[2] Tankha, Madhur, 'A Cracker of a Commercial', *The Hindu*, 4 January 2015

Those were the days when ads were a big part of the limited entertainment available. So, even though the ad was made on a limited budget, the jingle did well and so did the rabbit. Actually, so did Padhya who became something of a star, a sought-after for shows, events and parties.

The brand that started from a small housing society in Mumbai is now distributed not just across India but in many parts of the world including Asia, the Middle East, Europe and North America. Today, Lijjat has many branches which provide employment to tens of thousands of women across the country. Each person at Lijjat is a co-owner and an equal and the profits and losses of each of the branches are shared among the members of that branch. With its cooperative model, Lijjat has been a powerful example of a company that helps improve communities across India.

A truly *karram-kurram* tale. ('Hehehe!' the rabbit would have added.)

The Pulse Polio Campaign

Just as you thought The Angry Young Man, Amitabh Bachchan, had mellowed down, he began losing it again. The cause was non-filmi but explaining it requires that Bollywoodian cliché – a flashback.

Way back in the 1980s, one out of 100 babies in India was almost certain to get polio.[3] Crippled for life, these

[3] John, Jacob C., 'Two Years Without Polio', *The Hindu*, 13 June 2016

children would grow up physically disabled. As adults, many would find it impossible to find work.

In the 1990s, with development becoming a crucial goal, eradicating polio was at the top of the list. In 1995, when the Pulse Polio immunization programme began, it was seen as an investment in India's future. The government partnered with Rotary International, WHO, UNICEF and paediatricians across the country to put into place a set of measures to help eradicate this preventable disease. To ensure that every newborn was vaccinated, a mapping system was diligently followed. The target was to cover 100 per cent of children till the virus ran out of hosts.

Each immunization dose was made up of two drops of the vaccine and it was important to spread the message that just two drops could make life healthier. From 1995 to 2000, the immunization drive centred around the idea that: No child should be left out because all it took was '*do boond zindagi ki*'.

It was a message hammered into the consumer's brain through booklets, radio, television, newspaper ads, banners and wall paintings. People were continuously reminded of fixed polio vaccine days and camps through out-of-home media. All the ad lines were simple and matter-of-fact: 'Polio *ka koi ilaaj nahi, do boond har baar hai bachav sahi*' and '*Pehle paanch saal, mere bachchon ko do boond har baar*'.

With all the messaging and persuading, the number of reported polio cases started plunging. By 2000, the number reported was 265, a big drop from the two lakh cases per year in 1985.

And then, shockingly, the numbers started climbing again. In 2002, the number of reported cases had gone up to 1,556.

There seemed to be an absolutely unacceptable reason for this – people were actually resisting the immunization drive. It was obvious that cajoling was no longer working. Maybe it was time to show some anger.

And who would be a better candidate for that than the original Angry Young Man himself – Amitabh Bachchan?

So, by the end of 2002, Bachchan was sent to scold the masses. '*Sharm aani chaahiye humein!*' he said in his unmistakable voice in the television commercial. '*Laanat hai,*' he added, '*Hum mein se kuchh log apne bachhon ko* polio *ki dawa nahin pila rahein hain.*' He went on to ask people to listen carefully and ensure that not even one child remained unimmunized. Or else...(it would be a matter of great shame).[4]

Something clicked. The number of people bringing their children to the immunization booths began to rise. One woman reportedly even told a health officer at the booth that they didn't want to anger Amitabhji.

Thankfully, the number of polio cases began dropping again. As time went on, more stars lent their voice to the UNICEF Pulse Polio immunization programme – Shah Rukh Khan and Sachin Tendulkar among them.

---

[4] Vincent, Pheroze, 'When Amitabh's Voice Did the Trick to Make India Polio Free', *The Hindu*, 28 July 2014

The drive clearly worked, since the last case of polio was detected in Howrah, West Bengal, at the beginning of 2011. In 2014, India received polio-free status.

The Pulse Polio campaign is probably the biggest public health success story in the last few decades. It has become a story that's worth sharing. And it was the story shared by Bill Gates at the World Economic Forum in Davos, where he spoke about India's incredible success in making the country polio-free.

It is often cited as an example of a campaign that truly brought about change and made a difference. Even if, to begin with, it had seemed like just a drop (or two) in the ocean.

Chik Shampoo

It is not often that a company stresses about how a village is washing its tresses.

But that is exactly what Chik Shampoo did – and, in the process, gave the big MNC boys a manual on how to change consumer habits and sell your stuff.

First, let's go back to the beginning. Chinni Krishna owned a pharmaceutical products and cosmetics manufacturing and packaging company. His big idea? Packaging products in a way that they could be used just once. That is, selling things in sachets. This was an idea that encouraged trials and casual buying. He called sachets the product of the future.

It was Chinni Krishna's son, C.K. Ranganathan, today the CEO of CavinKare, who took the idea further. He realized that there was big rural market just waiting to be tapped. You see, in the 1980s, rural and small-town consumers used soap to wash their hair. Shampoo did not figure on their shopping list and was considered a luxury. To Ranganathan, this seemed like the perfect opportunity to turn the market on its huge, soapy head.

At 19, he had left the family business, which was controlled by his brothers, and set up his own company, Chik India (later renamed Beauty Cosmetics, which turned into CavinKare). By 1983, he had launched a shampoo called Chik and started selling it in little sachets.[5]

The grand idea was not just the sachet – it was the target audience. The company's focus was on the enormous rural market whose un-shampooed hair the MNCs were turning up their noses at. Chik shampoo was also looking to win friends among the lower middle-class, rural, semi-rural, mostly-female consumers.

In the beginning, though, there was no money for advertising. When it had to say something, the company simply printed its messaging on A4 sheets of paper. Rural audiences had to be shown how to use the shampoo – which included demonstrating the process live on boys (after which people were free to touch and smell their hair). And, of course, Chik shampoo

[5] Narasimhan, T.E., 'CavinKare does it again', *Business Standard*, 25 January 2013

sachets were distributed and made available to people for free. Brand activation is now a familiar term but the integration of consumer action through interaction and experience is what Chik did way back then.

As time went by, Chik Shampoo began sponsoring shows of mega-star Rajniknath's films. This allowed them to hold live demos for the film-goers and distribute free sachets to them. All this made for a marvellous run for the product in rural Tamil Nadu and Andhra Pradesh. By 1985, these promotional activities had helped sales jump an astonishing seven times over the previous year.

By 1989, the Chik sachets, priced at a very affordable ₹1, were very popular. The sachets were to be seen everywhere, were tiny and easy to pick up, and cost next to nothing. And, throughout this time, the company had kept innovating. At one point, it offered one new sachet in exchange for five used sachets of any shampoo, thus inducing trial. This campaign saw an immense response.

Their communication always showed a girl who had long, lustrous, de-tangled locks. In fact, a Chik line that became popular said, '*Yun kiya ho gaya*,' visualizing the easy-run-through of fingers through smooth hair. With wall paintings, video-on-wheels, door-to-door sampling and radio ads based on popular cinema dialogues, Chik kept weaning the rural consumer away from soap.

Just when prices seemed incapable of going lower or mass-ier, in 1999, the company introduced 4 ml sachets of cream-conditioning shampoo in five variants – Jasmine, Rose, Lily, Lavender and Petal. Each was priced at a very competitive 50 paise (other sachets were selling for as much as ₹2), which was aimed at making the price-to-value equation even more favourable among rural audiences.

By 2003, Chik shampoo was the second largest selling shampoo in the ₹1,200-crore (₹12 billion) shampoo market with a 21.4 per cent share, jostling with giants like HUL and P&G.[6]

Using brand activation techniques as an integral part of its innovative campaigns, the company had proved to be something of a tiny David *dho daalo*-ing ginormous Goliath heads. Sachet-ying all the way to the bank, Chik provided a compelling argument for little things going a long way.

Wheel

While we are accustomed to friends asking us to lend them our ears and loved ones asking us to give them 'missed calls', it was unexpected when Wheel detergent began asking folks to do both.

In 2012, HUL's Active Wheel detergent, popularly known as Wheel, wanted to do a campaign that focused on rural markets in UP, Bihar and Jharkhand. Penetration of communication channels in these areas was iffy, to say the least. Television viewing was not very prevalent in the more rural areas, and the areas that did have TV

[6] Lakshman, Nandini, 'The Big Small Brands Go for Gold', Rediff.com, 19 July 2003

often did not have dependable network connections, or electricity, for that matter. Low literacy rates made print an uncertain medium. And radio was too limited in its scope. This truly was the Bermuda Triangle as far as media reach was concerned.

Getting an idea often means making that metaphorical bulb light up. This time, though, the bulb was replaced by the screen of a cell phone.

Mobile phone penetration was something of a phenomenon in rural India around this time. As marketers quickly discovered, rural India had one thing in common with its urban counterpart – it relished mobile entertainment. Anecdotal evidence showed that people were even downloading songs and games on their phones by going to mobile recharge shops and that they were willing to pay for entertainment.

So Wheel's ad team got on to radio and gave people a very desi call-to-action. It encouraged them to give a 'missed call' from their phones to a specified number.

Wheel used the ubiquitous and unmistakably 'Indian' phrase: '*Zara* missed call *maarna*' to its own advantage with communication that said, 'Missed call *deejiye, muskuraate rahiye*.' Simple.

Once you called the given number and hung up, you would be called back and tickled with a helping of humour, the subject of which was often husbands, wives and marriage, a relatable theme for the consumer demographic of Wheel, and a theme it used extensively in its advertising. The content was customized in the language of the telecom circle that the number belonged to – for example, those in West Bengal would hear content in Bengali, and so on. The call included a brand message and an invitation to call again for more entertainment.

Wherever available, the number and call-to-action was reinforced on SMS, print and in-shop communication. Using the mobile phone as a push medium for integrated content worked for the rural markets Wheel was targeting and built solid recall for the brand.

In less than a month, the brand got about 1 lakh missed calls from 28,000 numbers. Months after launching the campaign in parts of UP and Bihar – hitherto considered media-dark – over 5 million missed calls had been received from 7.7 lakh numbers.

This was a milestone in advertising in many ways, and influenced many of the later campaigns Hindustan Unilever Limited carried out in these markets. In 2013, the company launched its Kan Khajura Tesan campaign, which told its consumers: 'Missed call *lagao, muft manoranjan pao*.'[7] This mobile platform provided free, on-demand entertainment on mobiles in rural areas, interspersed with ads of the company's brands: an idea that was clearly inspired by the success of the Wheel 'missed call' campaign.

Who knew a brand's call to action (in its communication) could be to miss connecting with it?

---

[7] Gangal, Ashwini, 'Kan Khajura Tesan: The Full Story', *afaqs!*, 30 June 2014

In the end, there are many pioneering examples of change-making that India has seen over the years. ITC's e-Choupal is an initiative that connects directly to local farmers over the Internet to procure produce. Sunfeast and Aashirvaad are just some of the brands that – along with farmers connected through them – the e-Choupal network helps sustain.

And whether or not they agreed, many decades ago, everyone would have been told by the Nirodh family planning campaign, '*Hum do, humaare do*'. Though the thought behind that campaign has since moved from having only two kids to spacing out births, for a whole generation, family planning was defined by that slogan and the red triangle that marked all the ads. It was one of the country's first social campaigns.

Whether motivated by social responsibility or plain old profitability, these trailblazers, along with many others, have impacted marketing and advertising and often brought about change – in thinking, practice or development. That's a lot of weight for a buck-toothed rabbit or a little blue-haired girl to carry, but they've done it and how!

Mummy Badnaam Hui

TARGETING CHARACTER ROLES

While most products could be argued to be gender-neutral, there are many ads that target a specific gender. Or stage in life. And many of these ads do so while showing said gender or stage in life itself.

Brands are here with a desirable product whatever the stage in life you may be in: mommy phase, kid phase, young-adult phase, I-kid-you-not-I'm-getting-my-navel-pierced phase, retirement phase, will-die-so-will-eat-sweets phase.

Tapping into consumer aspirations or playing on interpersonal dynamics sounds delicious to any marketer worthy of his target audience. On his blazer's padded shoulders lies the burden of ensuring that *that* consumer going through *that* stage feels the irresistible need for *that* particular product he happens to be selling.

The Woman

Not so long ago, popular media talked about women the way people talked about ghee – full of *shuddh* desi goodness. Today, they seem to be talking about women the way people now perceive ghee – a source of energy and rumoured to be a superfood. Women are the superheroines email forwards are forever saluting. Why, you ask? For holding down a job, cooking and running errands while taking care of the kids, the husband, the in-laws and their own good looks.

As some queen or the other observed in *Alice in Wonderland*, it takes all the running you can do just to remain in the same place.

Indian women have made their way to the top in corporate jobs, in international sports, in the political arena, as hot-shot lawyers and top-notch scientists. A woman of Indian origin has even made her way to outer space.

But, somehow, our ads show very few women who have made their way too far from the home. (In ads, women often only seem to be able to reach a stretch of a highway, all dressed to disco, waiting helplessly for a biker dude to roar to a stop and offer them a lift.) Ads are sometimes guilty of depicting women as commodities, pin-up girls, idols on a pedestal – whatever fits.

Many of these ads are addressing another target group – men. But while these depictions continue, it is becoming increasingly difficult to ignore today's women, who have to be advertised to as well. So sometimes, you also catch a glimpse of that aspirational figure – the free-ranging, forthright Indian woman. She talks about her periods, finds liberation through her microwave, scooter, sneakers, her cellular network, or her watch, finds *sachcha pyaar* with the perfect brand of lipstick and keeps away snotty, noisy babies with the help of over-the-counter pills. She has a job and therefore money to spend, not just on essentials but also on her lifestyle and on herself.

Spender, homemaker, persuader, decision-maker – it is becoming increasingly important for marketers to now talk to every kind of woman. But there is one particular kind who deserves a special mention – The Mummy.

Imagine you are a marketer. You have that magic-milk formula that transforms a bunch of runny-nosed toddlers into superheroes. Or maybe you have that pressure cooker that transforms *laukiwala dal* into a gourmet dish. The question is, have you managed to get that one person – that all-important person who can guarantee your product will knock all other products off shop shelves – on your side? Have you converted her, turned her into a loyal buyer of your product? Can you say, *mere paas maa hai*?

Yes, Mom Power is real.

Maa is a very strong character in our daily lives, homes and movies. She is shown to be of impeccable moral fibre, a tigress where her children are concerned and the pivot of the family. And if things don't go to plan, she starts crying.

For ages, moms in Bollywood movies wielded power by weeping. They wept through the 1950s, the 1960s and the 1980s.

To a casual observer, moms must have seemed incapable of taking charge. Yet, every movie buff understood that, weeping aside, the whole story centred on the sway she held over her son, the hero, who at some defining moment, in a voice rough with emotion said,

'*Mat ro, Maaaaaaaaaa!*' (At that point, the audience also started weeping.)

Likewise, the mother in ads often stayed a bit in the background, coming forward to serve nourishing milk-drinks, buy smarter detergents or cook healthy *pooris* in that healthier oil. But it was clear that she mattered. The marketer needed to catch her ear.

So it would be safe to go with the old saying that – '*Maa ka haath sar par hai toh* all is well.' But *maa ke haath mein aisa kya hai?*

Maa ke haath mein laydeez-purse *hai.* In fact, it is argued that the collective Indian-mommy spending power could equal a small nation's GDP.

Maa ke haath mein network *bhi hai.* Moms influence and look for advice from each other. The online world has opened up many avenues for communication. There are recommendations on Facebook and Twitter, bloggers referring to other bloggers, influencer moms as brand ambassadresses and buzzing comments sections below posts. It is obvious that moms like being talked with, not talked to. Opinions and reassurances are given on almost everything from the colour of their baby's poo to the state of the nation. And on many of these online platforms are ads. And product recommendations along with links to product pages.

For the marketer, it is a captivating gathering of the mummies– both as a character to be depicted and as an audience to tap.

Child

It's always been pretty obvious that in the provider-husband, nourisher-wife role-play that ads love so much, mummies have always been in charge when it comes to the good stuff that goes into kids, the gross stuff that comes out and all the stuff in between. In ads portraying 'typical' homes, it was always the mummies who made the decisions, changed the diapers, packed the tiffin boxes, dispensed Dettol and free advice, and influenced the kids' every activity.

Then one day the winds of change huffed and puffed and blew that home down.

No sooner did this happen than marketers got a whiff of it. 'Mummies are just not cutting it anymore,' they gossiped. They recognized instantly that it was the kids with minds of their own and peer-group lifestyles to imitate who were making the choices. Pester-power was now stronger than ever before, and strong-willed kids could wear down their mummies (and daddies) into getting them almost anything they felt the need to possess. What's more, the league of superbrats knew instinctively of that all-consuming parental disorder – GUILT. So they concocted the perfect formula:

Pester power + guilt = opportunity to acquire new things

In effect, this left the all-powerful, all-decision-making mummy's reputation in shreds. And that is how mummy *badnaam hui, darrling tere liye.*

Savvy marketers (many driven by the debatable intention of 'catching them young' and keeping them loyal for life) had found a new target audience with massive potential ripe for the capture.

Man

These kids running around in ads, they almost always seem to be products of Immaculate Conception. The mummies are visible but *where is the dad*? In our ads, the man rarely hangs with (or hovers over) the kids. Instead, he worries about insurance, asks '*Kitna deti hai?*' about cars, sometimes brushes his teeth and tears up when his daughter gets married. Oh, and once in a long while, he loads the washing machine.

If anyone asked this guy, '*Kitne aadmi thhe?*,' he would wearily tell him *ki bhai*, there were too many to count. Apart from being a dad, the man is under pressure to be well, many kinds of man – family man, party boy, the man with a plan. (And Shah Rukh acquiring six-pack abs and doing 'Dard-e-Disco' in his forties hasn't made things any easier.)

In the 1990s, you were no longer merely separating the men from the boys. You were separating the pedicured, moisturized men from the ungroomed, bushy-browed ones. A new term was emblazoned across the horizon – 'metrosexual'. Like Beckham, the metrosexual icon of the time, these guys were bending the rules. They wanted to be well-groomed and dared to do something about it.

But times and terms are flexible. Metrosexuals were different from the retrosexuals – those beer and cricket-loving, old-fashioned guys who couldn't care less about the way they looked. If there was no beer, they'd have a *shikanji*, with added sugar, please (none of that sugar-free frippery, thank you). Then there were the ubersexuals, holding up the fort for all that is good and male. And smelling nice while they were at it.

Whatever the term that came to life and then faded, what was common was that men themselves were intrigued by these identities and the *bahut saarey aadmi* that they could be. There had been enough of women wanting to be more than someone's daughter, sister, wife, mother. Men, too, wanted to be more than bread-earning sons, husbands, dads and grandpas. They wanted to be *matrosaxxy*. Or *ratrosaxxy*. Or just *hatro-saxxy*.

And so, also part of some family, of course, but shown lone-rangering, is the red-blooded Indian male. He is the one who thinks a lot about razors and fresh breath, rides bikes or cool cars and is known to seduce the lady next door with the irresistible whiff of his very-very-affordable deodorant.

Ads also have place for some 'character roles'. While the '*Grenpa*' has been typecast into sitting around, reading newspapers and enjoying his insurance-enriched life, the smart, adorable *nani* acts as the keeper of all the Ayurvedic know-how in the family. (There's Ramu *kaka* too, forever holding a red-checked gamchha and talking about *jalebi* or *garam* roti but he is mostly the 'extra'.)

So there you have it – just some of the metamorphosing characters that make up the cast or are the target audiences of in the ad stories that follow.

Maggi Noodles

The Indian's love for Chinese food goes back many decades. It is a love so transformative that we now make 'Chinese' dishes that do not exist in China. Veg Manchurian or chilli paneer anyone? Or would you rather have an American Chopsuey (a special treat not to be found either in China...or America for that matter)?

So when instant noodles were launched in India, it was done on the safe assumption that people would take to it without doubt or hesitation, that it would be an instant hit.

It was not.

In 1982, Nestlé India Limited launched Maggi 2-Minute Noodles, a first-of-its-kind product for India. Maggi was first targeted at a much older, more attractive-sounding consumer segment – the working woman (this was some years before the superbrats' superpowers had been sussed out by marketers). Advertised as a quick-to-prepare, delicious meal-in-a-bowl, Maggi 2-Minute Noodles was positioned as the perfect alternative to cooking at the end of a long day.

The product did not do well. Apparently women rejected the promise of a ready meal that made life easier on a weeknight. India was then a country with conservative food habits and, even with much advertising thrown into the mix, Maggi's sales showed no signs of picking up. Perplexed, Nestlé conducted a research study and was taken aback by a key finding. Their instant noodles, it appeared, were quite popular with a new consumer segment in town – kids. Even though the product promise was not directed at them, they were slurping up the noodles.

For Nestlé, it was straight back to school. Unceremoniously dumping the ungrateful working woman, it focused on kids and began promoting Maggi with the child consumer in mind. This time, the company got its act right. It distributed free samples to children, both packaged and cooked. The children loved the noodles and soon enough more and more households started stocking up on Maggi Noodles.

When Maggi advertised, it showed kids in easy-to-identify-with situations like rushing in from play even as the song played in the background – *'khel-kood ke jab bhi aayein, chahe harein chahe haraayen...'*

Maggi Noodles was presented as the solution to the eternal wail, 'Mummy, *bhookh lagi hai*!' And the Mummy responded, unfazed, 'Bas, *do* minute!' and instantly provided a fun dish for the kids to wolf down. Everyone agreed that the 2-minute noodles were 'Fast to cook! Good to eat!'

To add to the ads, Nestlé ensured that the product's engagement level with kids was kept high. It offered them gifts in exchange for empty packs they returned to stores. At one time, there was quite an aspirational Maggi Club with a venerated president who went by the name of Mr Doodle Dee. In return for logo cut-outs from packs, kids received assorted fun stuff and membership into the group of 'Maggi Clubbers, fun lovers'.

Over time, the company tried to keep their customers' tastebuds involved with innovations. It introduced new variants and flavours like chicken, tomato and sweet-and-sour. Some will remember Maggi Sweet and Maggi Chaat, and there was Maggi Soup Style as well. Many of the variants gradually disappeared, except for one hot little number – the Maggi Cuppa. The noodles that could be prepared in and eaten from its own container.

By the late 1980s, it became evident that the category Maggi Noodles had created, and now owned, was huge. By 2014, the market for instant noodles, which had been non-existent in 1982, was estimated to be worth over ₹2,000 crore.[1] By then, tempted by the size of the pie (or portion of noodles), other brands tried edging in – ITC's Yippee, HUL's Knorr, GSK's Foodles and Nissin's Top Ramen.

But, till 2014, it was Maggi that ruled the roost with about three-fourth of the instant noodle market in India, which was in any case its biggest market. Today, Maggi is

[1] Karnik, Madhura, 'Charted: How Maggi Rules India's Noodle Market', *Quartz*, 5 June 2015

commonly available at your local *thelawala* (customized to requests like, 'Maggi *dena, mirch maar ke*'), in restaurant menus (Thai-style fusion Maggi!) and, of course, in your kitchen, garnished with *anda-bhurji*. Almost everyone has a favourite Maggi recipe or story to share and every person who has lived in a hostel at any point in his or her life will vouch for its soul-reviving quality. To maintain an emotional connect with generations that have grown up on Maggi, the company even has a web page full of consumer testimonials and stories shared by a nostalgic generation. Its Maggi's way of holding on to the now – 'old' faithfuls.

The distinctive yellow packaging, the brand name and colouring and the distinctive sound of 'Maggi!' being uttered are inseparable associations with the brand. Today, the biggest testimony to the box office success of Maggi's marketing-masala mix is that the name Maggi has become synonymous with instant noodles.

And with its popularity, it is safe to assume that right now, someone somewhere is having a plate of Maggi.

McDonald's

All 'convent-school' types have sung this song (though maybe not in these words):

Old Mack Dawn-ald had a farm, E, I, E, I, O.
And on that farm he had some aloo, E, I, E, I, O.
With an aloo patty here and an aloo tikki burger there...

Yes, we have replaced the cows with aloo...quite like McDonald's has done in its Indian outlets. In 1989, when the company was tentatively checking out the Great Indian Opportunity, the scenario may have seemed pretty bleak to them. After all, a brand known for its iconic beef burgers entering a country where cows are worshipped? Holy cow!

In addition, the fast-food industry and the retail market was in its infancy and had very few standardized practices. Not only did McDonald's have to adapt to the taste preferences of local consumers, it also had to sort out supply and distribution issues.

As a result, the company took its time, a few years actually, to establish its back-end operations and begin business. It used the time to set up a supply chain that would ensure consistent quality, and it devised refrigeration and storage solutions for different ingredients to guarantee standardized flavours.

But, most importantly, McDonald's had to close the door on its past, open the door to the future, take a deep breath and consider being a part-time vegetarian. To get the consumer to push the brand's beefy reputation to the back of their minds, they decided to come up with '*shuddh veg*' options that were even handled separately in the kitchen.

In 1996, McDonald's finally launched its restaurants in India and revolutionized food retailing in the country. A McDonald's counter became just a stage for presenting the final product of a huge chain industriously at work. By 2011, the company had established itself as the market leader, one of the most successful fast-food franchises in

India. Apart from providing amazing value-for-money and a family eating-out experience that assured tasty, trendy meals for every generation, they also dabbled in home delivery. For a chain known across the world for its beef burgers, the Indian vegetarian burger has had a wonder-item status in their profile.

Many other factors also contributed to its success, not least among them were the little factors – the children – forming the fast food giant's core target audience. Now, few things make a marketer happier than an unhappy child, because chances are that if buying something can make the kid happy, the parent will buy it. The terrible twos (and threes, fours, fives...you get the drift) that babies go through, with all the tears and wailing and stamping of feet and rolling on the floor? Some believe they spend those years simply training their parents for a lifetime of being on their toes. But marketers are on their toes the minute there's a kid in the picture, acting on research that has shown that if they sweet-talk a kid into listening, they will have a faithful customer for life. Apparently, during the very time that they are throwing tantrums and wearing down their parents, they are really listening very attentively to marketers. The little traitors!

McDonald's used this knowledge quite masterfully in its 1997 television commercial. It showed a little boy shyly walking on to the school stage to recite a poem...only to find himself frozen. Daddy, who is in the audience, decides to take the stricken child to McDonald's (Mummy, while there, was a bit of a prop in this case). In that warm, familiar happy space, the child found nourishment and his voice. Sitting on a table, he recited the whole poem cheerily to applause from the entire restaurant.

Knowing that brand loyalty can begin even at the age of two, McDonald's had global experience in the art of targeting the very young. And they were successful too because, for many kids, sitting with Ronald McDonald – the grinning 'Chief Happiness Officer' of the brand – on the bench outside a McDonald's outlet was almost up there with meeting Santa Claus at the mall. Then there was the McDonald's Happy Meal. When yet-to-be-literate toddlers began pointing at the Golden Arches – the big golden 'M' that marked out a McDonald's counter – and throwing tantrums till they got a Happy Meal, you had to wonder what they were more interested in, the burger or the gift, and marvel at the genius of the marketing. The McDonald's Happy Meal typically packed in a burger, a coke and a toy. Interestingly, if ordered separately, the food might have cost less, but it was the toy that made the decision a no-brainer for parents, because a Happy Meal = Happy Kid = Happy Parents.

While, worldwide, the Happy Meal was perhaps not considered a major money-spinner, the overwhelming response it got in India made it a wildly successful strategy. It kept customers hooked. McDonald's replaced the toy regularly and spent money marketing every new toy in-store and in the media. In fact, McDonald's was known to be the world's largest distributor of toys, with one toy included in every 15 per cent of its sales![2] (Which is probably why brands like the home-grown Nirula's tried a Buddy Meal too. It got a great response but could not manage the recall that the Happy Meal seemed to generate.)

In 2016, twenty years after it first opened in India, McDonald's celebrated with a commercial that showed its journey. It showed a teenaged boy and girl in one of McDonald's first restaurants in India. The girl is shown rummaging around for her toy in her Happy Meal box. The boy spots it fallen on the floor and gives it to her. Thus begins a bond that lasts through the years, with McDonald's remaining the go-to place for the two of them to visit even as the world around them kept changing. It ends with the two of them celebrating their son's birthday at McDonald's and, surprise, suprise, with their son meeting a girl just like they had. 'A lot has changed. Nothing has changed,' the brand told you.

Sure enough, even in the real world, the restaurant is frequented by a lot of children, of course, but by families and young couples as well. With over 400 restaurants across India, McDonald's serves over 320 million people annually.[3]

---

[2] Nudelman, Mike, Ashley Lutz, '12 Facts About McDonald's That Will Blow Your Mind', *Business Insider*, 15 April 2015

[3] 'McDonald's Celebrates its 20 Years in India With a New Brand Campaign', *afaqs!*, 9 November 2016

But even as the burger grew on the tot and the tot grew up, so did the market. And the number of players. Today, apart from KFC and Dunkin' Donuts (both of which sell burgers), Wendy's, Fat Burger, Johnny Rocket and Jack in the Box have all set up shop in the country.

McDonald's traditional rival Burger King, which opened in India towards the end of 2014, generated an average of ₹3.1 crore from each of its outlets in the FY 2015–16. Meanwhile, McDonald's posted average sales of ₹3.6 crore from each of its outlets in the same year.[4]

The year 2017 brought with it some problems. Several outlets had to down their shutters because of licensing issues that some attribute to long-standing legal tussles in management.

But much before all this, even before the arch-rivals arrived on the scene, there was already an influx of desi offerings. Indianized outlets like 'Burger Singh' were trying to tickle our imagination with burgers called 'Jatt Putt', 'Bihari Gosht' and 'Achaari Mutton'.

Thing is, Burger Singh may or may not get to be king but all this must put much pressure on McDonald's.

But then it *is* old McDonald's. There's sure to be a bun or two (or a million) in the oven.

---

[4] Tyagi, Neha, 'Affordable Pricing Helps Burger King Log Rs 141 Crore in Sales', *Economic Times*, 9 December 2016

Ariel Matic

There was a time was when a Bollywood hero told his heroine things like '*Chunri sambhaal gori, udee chali jaaye.*' Or '*Laaga chunri mein daag.*' At which point, you itched for the heroine to turn around, spit on the ground and say, '*Toh? Tumhein dhona padega kya?*'

Really serious studies suggest that forget *chunris*, a woman herself can take flight into space and return home to her husband only to find the laundry waiting to be done. Men just don't want to hang out with the wash and the detergent.

In 2012, the market for detergents in India was slated by those-in-the-know as having the potential to grow to over ₹24,000 crore in the next five years.[5] It was a market that had been growing at about 14 per cent a year in value though volume growth was lower. Price hikes (and wars) accounted for lower industry margins.

Three variants of detergents were popular in the country – bar detergents, liquid detergents and powder detergents. Among these, powder detergents had always ruled the roost and had widespread acceptance. The industry comprised an organized sector and an unorganized one. The organized sector was the larger one, with players like HUL, Rohit Surfactants, P&G, Nirma and Jyothy Laboratories. These companies owned

---

[5] Bhupta, Malini, 'Soaps and Detergents Market Sees Plenty of Action', *Business Standard*, 24 January 2013

the most visible brands that we see. Depending on their price, the brands themselves belonged to three detergent sub-categories – the economy range, with brands like Ghari, Nirma and Wheel; the mid range, with brands like Tide, Rin and Mr White; and the premium range, with Surf Excel, Henko and Ariel.

Ariel was launched by P&G in India in 1991. Since then it had fought for its turf with product variants, pricing strategies and the tom-tomming of 'technology' as a magic ingredient. It had created ad campaigns for its products, well aware that advanced cleaning properties were best noticed when there was some emotional appeal involved.

Their core target, women, they knew, did not easily buy into a detergent's claims of having cleaning technology superior to a rival product. They were known, rather, to buy into brands that they came across on the family or peer-group grapevine. Tapping into their aspirations and becoming part of their conversations was more likely to yield results.

This then became integral to Ariel's marketing mix when, in 2015, it wanted to advertise for Ariel Matic, specifically made for fully and semi-automatic washing machines. The product had technology that not only helped clean but was also ruthless on *daag-dhabbas*.

The brand had of late supported a Nielsen study on Indian households. The findings had proven that the Indian male's sense of gender-equality was itself a big *dhabba* on his fair species. It showed that 76 per cent of men believed that doing the laundry was a woman's job.[6]

Meanwhile, women perceived the roles of men and women to be unequal at home. They knew of women who, just like men, were politicians, actresses, bankers, journalists, astronauts, businesswomen, scientists and army personnel. But unlike men, they felt that between office and the home, women had to work two jobs. 'Work' for men was just office. (That is, only the husband could sing '*Main tera* (x4) Hero No. 1' inside the home, no matter what the heroine was achieving outside in the world.)

While it was all right for him to put up his feet after a long day, she needed to take care of the housekeeping. These behaviour patterns and mindsets were deep-rooted, often in both genders.

Laundry, in particular, seemed unquestionably a woman's job. As far as Ariel Matic was concerned, this was clearly an opportunity to do some couples' counselling. In public.

Their 'Share the Load' campaign did just that. The underlying force was a detergent so superior and yet so simple to use that the wash-load had no option but to turn out perfectly clean, whoever loaded the machine, the wife or the husband.

So exactly why was it that men did not contribute to household work? This was the question Ariel asked,

[6] Singh, Namrata, 'Two-thirds of Women Say Men Don't Help With Household Chores: Study', *Times of India*, 9 January 2015

using laundry as a metaphor for all the chores around the house.

As part of its communication, there was a television commercial which showed two older women having tea at home. Even as they discussed the changing times and the number of women heading out to work, the *bahu* of the house was seen getting ready to leave for office. Just as the *saas* was heard revealing delightedly that her daughter-in-law earned more than her son, the son called out, asking his wife why his green shirt hadn't been washed.

Pause (a fully pregnant one at that).

Then the commercial ended with a super asking, 'Is laundry only a woman's job?', followed by the campaign hashtag #ShareTheLoad.[7]

Ariel wanted to give a movement-like feel to the campaign and gather emotional equity. So it employed every tool imaginable to drive the point home – news channels, opinion leaders, celebrities, bloggers and all kinds of influencers debated the issue of the sharing of chores and invited chatter around it.

The pack aimed at making laundry more approachable for men and a fun activity for couples.

A few washing-machine manufacturers helped endorse the Ariel stance. Some brands and designers featured clothes carrying tags with the message 'This fabric can be washed by both men and women.'

---

[7] https://www.youtube.com/watch?v=JCnoAQVy_8E

Even the *dabbawalas* of Mumbai were roped into delivering the message to office-workers along with their lunch, the T-shirts they wore bearing the message as well.

Adoption and participation were key elements of the campaign. On the brand page and on social-media feeds, women were encouraged to share the different ways in which they were communicating the 'Share the load' message to the men in the house.

Ad recall remained high as many people engaged with the brand. The result seemed to be that laundry, while still not irresistibly attractive to Indian men, appeared to become more approachable.

In 2016, Ariel Matic got Irrfan Khan to show up at the launch of a #ShareTheLoad pack (which proposed laundry on odd days for him and even days for her)[1]. Then came another Ariel '#SharetheLoad' commercial. In it, a father watched his daughter come home from work, look after her child, make tea for her husband and put dinner on the table. He then composed a letter of apology to his daughter. In that, he talked about how he himself had never challenged patriarchal attitudes to housework and so his daughter grew up playing 'house-house' and not questioning the fact that housework had become her job. He swore to change, and was seen back in his house, sharing the load of the laundry with his wife. The film ended with the question: 'Why is laundry only the mother's job?' and the hashtag, #DadsShareTheLoad.

Sheryl Sandberg, the chief operating officer (COO) of Facebook, shared the video on her platform, saying it was one of the most powerful videos she had seen – showing how stereotypes hurt everyone and were passed on from generation to generation. She pointed out that when little girls and boys play house, they model their parents' behaviour and this doesn't just impact their childhood games, it shapes their long-term behaviour. Within hours, her post was shared thousands of times, earning enormous goodwill for Ariel's call to action.

The campaign also topped the annual World Advertising Research Centre's (WARCs) 100 ranking which ranks the world's best marketing campaigns and companies according to the business impact of their marketing strategies. WARC stated that through the campaign more than 1.5 million men pledged to share household chores and the campaign helped Ariel more than double its value and volume in sales, which grew 106 per cent and 105 per cent, respectively, in that very year.[8]

Like all good stories, 'Share the load' was an idea that kept showing its potential long after it was first articulated. Much like the filmy *chunris* of our hero-heroines in the beginning of this story, it took wing.

Havells Home Appliances

Clearly in couples' therapy, it's the man who needs all the counselling. This is because, apart from not doing

---

[8] 'P&G's Ariel tops WARC 100', WARC, 4 April 2017

Tewari, Saumya, 'Ariel's 'Share the Load' Campaign Tops WARC Advertising Ranking', *Livemint*, 4 April 2017 anything in the laundry department (as mentioned in the example before this), apparently he doesn't do much in the kitchen either.

This is what Havells set out to change.

Tackling the socially pertinent route in a light manner in its communication was pretty much a Havells thing. In 2013, their ad campaign, '*Hawa badlegi*' talked about the winds of change and one of the ads showed the husband taking on his wife's surname after marriage.

At the time, Havells India was a 7,000-crore electrical goods and power distribution equipment maker[9] and it was looking at more-than-doubling its market share, in the next couple of years, in the home appliances segment.

Appliances for the home? That place where there were helpless male creatures who couldn't boil an egg, leave alone juice a carrot? How about telling them of gadgets which were so easy to use that men needn't depend on their women to survive the daily grind.

Havells' products included a mixer grinder, juicer, iron, coffee-maker and air-fryer. All of the products could be used in the house by anybody. But all of them were typically perceived as being handled solely by women because such stuff was a woman's job, you know. Havells took on this viewpoint with gusto. It was made absolutely clear – Havells kitchen appliances were gender-neutral products and a man could use the appliances just as much

---

[9] 'Havells to Set Up Rs 50-Cr Manufacturing Unit in Rajasthan', *The Hindu Business Line*, 4 October 2013

as a woman could. Taking a step out of the kitchen? Very much so. A step away from conventions thrust upon women? Yes, that too.

So in 2014, Havells released a campaign which said, 'Respect women'.

The brand ran a series of television commercials all based on the idea that a woman is not a kitchen/ general small appliance herself. Even though this was a subject that could evoke much strife, the ad films themselves took a humorous tone.

One of the commercials opened on a typical arranged-marriage scenario where the family of the 'boy' had come to see the prospective bride in her house. The boy's mother is seen chatting about how life was so difficult for him in the USA, how he needed to settle down because, really, how long could he keep going out just to get a cup of coffee? The girl, hearing this, gives a smile and leaves the room only to return with a Havells coffee-machine. She then suggests that he settle down with the appliance instead, since she was not a coffee-maker.

Another film showed a man getting ready for work when he notices that his shirt had not been ironed. Mentioning that he was the head of a team and could not go to work dressed in an unironed shirt, he asks his wife to iron it for him. She hands him a Havells iron, saying that his team would probably not like a boss who did not know how to iron his own shirt. She points out that the appliance was an *istree* (an iron) while she was a *stree* (a woman).

Yet another commercial showed a woman serving idlis and chutney to her husband. While relishing the fare, he finds it necessary to tell her that his mother would have made three different kinds of chutney. His wife steps away and comes back with the Havells mixer-grinder for him to make chutney with. She then tells him that she was his wife, his *patni*, not a maker of *chutney* (or *chatni*).

Another film showed a man eyeing a neighbour doing yoga on her terrace. When his wife notices this, he begins talking about how the neighbour probably cooked healthy food. The wife gets him the Havells air-fryer, which cooked healthy food too. She tells him that it was something he could marry and then be at liberty to watch the neighbour.

And then there was the film which opened on a man returning from the tennis courts with a friend. They feel like having some fresh juice and the man asks his wife to make some. She hands him a carrot, an orange and the Havells juicer while introducing herself to the friend as the wife of the man who saw her as a kitchen appliance.

These 'respect women' ads were quite noticeable, much more so than the usual commercials in the category which had a roll-call of product features – something people did not really want to watch as far as small appliances were concerned.

Plus, there was little to differentiate products, so connecting with end-users was a good bet. The ads showcased the functionality of the products while showing them in a broader perspective – as user-gender independent.

To add to this, the ads were also aired during the IPL season in 2014. This ensured high visibility with a sizeable male audience while expectedly, women empathized with the ads anyway. The ads were designed to make people aware of their deep-seated conditioning but they were also witty and sharply thought–provoking. Catchy takeaways like *stree-istree* and *patni-chatni* made them stick in the minds of consumers.

Apart from television, the marketing plan included print, digital, radio and point-of-sale material. By May 2014, Havells was prolifically seen on social media where the communication had been well-received. It had also teamed up with Culture Machine, a digital video entertainment company, to create a music video.[10]

Here the percussionist, Sarthak, is seen sitting with a male friend and trying to create a tune. When another friend, a woman (Vasudha from pop band, Aasma), tries to help, he gets annoyed and in that timeless put-down to women, tells her to go to the kitchen and make him a sandwich(!).

She does go to the kitchen, where she begins to compose music using kitchen appliances. Soon, he can't help but join in too. The music beats turned out to be an innovative blend of A.R. Rahman's '*Humma Humma*' and sounds created by showcasing Havells appliances (the sweet noise of whirrrr, grrroooomm and pfshaww).

---

[10] Sen, Satrajit, 'Havells Creates #RespectForWomen Online', *afaqs!*, 2 June 2014

Basically, for three minutes, the video stayed true to the thought that a woman's place was not in the kitchen. It was wherever she wanted it to be. And this was illustrated, literally, by a woman making music in the kitchen. And then, by the woman asking the man to make her a sandwich in said kitchen.

The video was uploaded on Being Indian, a YouTube channel that features uniquely Indian videos. Later, Havells uploaded it on its own YouTube channel and on its Facebook and Twitter pages. Within 24 hours, the video had got thousands of views.

The fact that the campaign struck such a chord made its message really clear – give R-E-S-P-E-C-T, or get it ground, juiced or ironed out of you.

AND.

Make your own sandwich.

Raymond

The Indian male doesn't belong in a suit. He belongs in suiting and shirting. Or so our suiting-shirting ads keep telling us.

It is not just the marketers singing the suiting-shirting song who keep a lascivious watch on the consumer's dress sense. It is this dress sense that decides the food, clothing and employment prospects of over 45 million people directly and 60 million people indirectly. The Indian textiles industry is an employer so gargantuan, it cannot be ignored by anyone. In fact, in almost a nod to the Bollywood-inspired phrase – roti, *kapda aur makaan*, it is second only to agriculture. Estimated to be over US $108 billion in 2015, the textile industry was expected to grow to US $223 billion in the next ten years. It contributed about 4 per cent to India's GDP, and 14 per cent to the overall Index of Industrial Production (IIP).[11]

The industry is not without its complexities, which includes an inherent ruthlessness towards those not quite tailored for survival. Hugely capital intensive, it is also very competitive. In the arena are innumerable players from both the organized as well as the unorganized sector.

In this context, while there have been many established brands constantly trying a *cheerharan* of sorts on each other, namely Vimal, OCM, Siyaram, Digjam, Mayur, Dinesh and Donear, the Raymond brand has been remarkably successful. Surviving the suiting game since 1925, it still looks sharp sitting on top of the worsted textiles market with a 60 per cent share.

In the 1980s, star cricketers from the Indian national team told you, one after another, that there was 'Only Vimal', and Indians cosied up instantly to the sales pitch. After all, it was the charismatic West Indian Vivian Richards and the home-grown charmer, bowler Ravi Shastri, they were listening to. Digjam got the suave film-maker Shekhar Kapur to pose for them, while Sunil Gavaskar dressed up in Dinesh Suiting and 'Tiger' Pataudi

---

[11] Bathla, Seema, Prateek Kukreja, 'How to Get the Weave Right', *The Hindu*, 21 July 2016

was the face for Gwalior Suitings or Grasim. Meanwhile, Raymond presented people with its 'guide to the well-dressed man' projecting sophistication as their image.

Come 1992 and the word 'metrosexual' was being bandied around. Superficially, at least, people were warming up to the idea of a *metrosexy mard* who felt some *dard*. The angry young man had been a crowd-puller, but what's not to like about a guy who wants a *chumma* on a *jumma*?

Your Raymond guy would never dream of demanding a kiss quite that boisterously but it was a good space to be in. Raymond put together a winning strategy and a winner of a guy as the face of its campaign. He was no cricketer, film star or film director. He wasn't even notional royalty. They called him 'The Complete Man'.

The time was just right. People were used to the portrayal of male aggression and superiority in visual media of all kinds. But 'The Complete Man' in Raymond ads was not quite like any man they had seen before.

Over the years, he has been the guy who impulsively danced at a wedding sangeet, the 'boy' who made a reluctant candidate for an arranged marriage feel comfortable, the young man who took special care of an old school teacher who was feeling awkward at a gathering and the husband who took care of the baby as his wife left home for work.

The ads told you he did not shy away from emotions. He was a family guy and, yes, sensitive and vulnerable. He was a great dad, sometimes a good friend, always a non-Alpha-male husband...and, boy, did he look good in his Raymond suit.

This was someone the urban, well-off man thought he would like to be, and soon The Complete Man became so saleable that the ads often left out product shots. Yes, he even made ads complete just by being there. The idea struck a chord across socio-economic groups. While the target audience was the upper middle class, Raymond found buyers across strata. This was largely because the brand steered away from being elitist. It kept as its core the elements of emotions and relationships, which are essentially similar across the world. In that sense, this was a really big idea. What made it even bigger was the fact that it did not depict the guy who bought the product. It just showed the kind of guy he might like or aspire to be.

The campaign was enormously successful – enough for the other suits to sit up and take note. Over the decades, some other brands signed on celebrities to differentiate themselves and some tried to introduce the metrosexual angle to their ads too. Gwalior Suitings brought in Mansoor Ali Khan Pataudi's celebrity wife Sharmila Tagore and celebrity son Saif Ali Khan to join him in their ads and add to the *khandani*-celeb status of the brand. In the ad developed by Mayur Suitings, Shah Rukh Khan was 'Mayur' Khan, an actor who was a 'family man'. OCM showed the wife noticing the husband only when he changed into an OCM suit, with what sounded like 'O see him' partly playing in the background.

Whatever the competition came up with, Raymond remained the name memorably associated with The

Complete Man positioning. Today, it is counted as one of the largest makers of worsted suiting fabric.

Apart from its distinctive advertising, Raymond engages with consumers on social media like Facebook. It uses the platform to connect with customers and keep itself top-of-mind. The heritage brand from 1925 does this by either putting up regular, modern styling tips on its page or with activities like model hunts.

But whatever it is that consumers look towards Raymond's for, the strength of its positioning remains in the words – the complete man. Because you never can quite be the complete man. You can only aspire to be one. So charmer, dad, fiancé, husband – the complete man has always been every kind of a man.

Oh, till 2016. When he became a woman.

Yes, in a one-off Raymond complete man ad, 'he' was actually a 'she' – a single mom – whose son gifts her a 'world's best dad' mug on Father's Day.

Daddy cool?

Or woman: without her, man is incomplete?

Or whatever, as long as everybody loves Raymond?

18 Again

When Madonna sang about feeling 'like a virgin', she probably never imagined that, close to two decades later, an Indian home maker clad in a sari would be singing the tune meaningfully – not because she was inspired by the song, but because she now had the means to make her vagina literally feel, well, 18 Again.

In 2012, pharmaceutical company Ultratech India launched 18 Again, a vaginal rejuvenation and tightening gel. It was positioned in the personal-care space or, more accurately, in the women's personal-care space. It was showcased as a health product with medical benefits and launched as a first-of-its-kind, completely herbal product for use by women of all ages, from puberty to menopause.

With ingredients such as pomegranate, aloe vera, gold and Vitamin E, it claimed it could remove dead tissue, improve blood circulation and keep the vagina hydrated, toning the area and giving it more elasticity.

When 18 Again entered the market, it was not the first product in the vaginal space. There were washes like Lactacyd, Ayur's Hygiene Wash, Tulip Personal Wash. There was also a whole range of products from Clean & Dry Intimate – a burn and itch cream, a powder for controlling wetness and a body-wash that would refresh the vagina.

There had even been a vaginal whitening cream that had provoked much controversy around women being made to feel inadequate yet again. But it was conceivably a product that men too could have surreptitiously used to get *gora-chitta* down there. With 18 Again, there was no such debate. So focused was the product promise that it was unmistakably targeted at women.

Men have always been told that as far as the Olympics in Bed were concerned, they could become faster, higher, stronger by using certain products. But no one had clearly stated this to women as yet. So, what if a female hygiene product like 18 Again could help a woman enhance her sexuality and celebrate it?

The thought the marketers arrived at was 'Feel like a virgin'. According to them, the kind of woman who could celebrate her sexuality was a virgin(?). (Quite contrary, this.)

The product was launched in a celebrity-studded event, featuring women of stature known for their strong views on the empowerment of the gender. Among others, the actress, Celina Jaitley, a vocal advocate of women's issues was present along with Mahabanoo Kotwal, known for her stellar performance in the Indian version of Eve Ensler's *Vagina Monologues*. No coy *log* here. As a panel talked about empowerment and the societal silence about problems women face every day. Since it was a rejuvenating cream for the vagina, the word cropped up frequently during the discussion.

The word itself and the issues being addressed rarely came up in public, so the crafting of the communication had its challenges. The product category was 'sensitive', so the messaging needed to be engaging without making consumers uncomfortable. Besides, the product benefit had to be conveyed through sanitized imagery to avoid controversy and other hassles. And that is how Madonna became a Munni.

The lyrics of Madonna's song seemed to tick many boxes. While the connection with the product was obvious, the words also negated the possibility that the cream could be mistaken for an anti-ageing application or any other kind of beauty product.

When the television commercial was aired, it was clearly centered on the feeling of being a virgin – again.

Health was not the central thought in the communication. There was no skin shown in the ads. In fact, the woman in the ad was wrapped in a sari. This was a woman with children, just like the women the company was targeting.

The ad film told the story in a household setting, opening in a traditional home milling with family members, somewhere in southern India. A lady was seen walking out to the courtyard as her husband was about to leave for work – only to be waylaid by his wife who then led him into a dance, singing, 'I feel like a virgin.' Oh, did we mention the place was milling with family members? Obviously, she taught them a thing or two because the film ended with our Madonna-Munni's mother-in-law logging into the 18 Again website as her husband smiles down at her. (Maybe breathlessly planning a sequel?)

The product launch was followed by on-ground efforts such as interactive sessions with gynaecologists in malls. But before much could happen, in fact almost immediately after the launch, the ad and the product became the centre of debate.

Some felt that the virginal and 18-ager aspirations of the women portrayed in the ads eclipsed any claims about health and hygiene. Others argued that instead of showing the empowerment of women, the ads were feeding women's insecurities.

Conspiracy theorists wondered that if the product worked, who would it benefit more – women or men? Could it be that the company's aim was actually to get men interested in the end result and therefore pressurize their women to use the product?

Such opinions and discussions became the subject of much social media attention. While some thought the ad to be provocative but (at least) without objectionable imagery, others found it cringe-worthy and an addition to the burden of expectations women already had to deal with.

In general, though, the critics drowned out the pro-empowerment voices.

Today, the product still exists and though it was such a clearly targeted product, it did not see as much success as anticipated. The 18 Again Facebook page only has posts from the year it was launched in which is when it was most talked about. Social media chatter around it sometimes still surfaces, giving an indication of the reactions the ad had induced:

'A vaginal tightening cream? Let me do *ulti* and come back.'

'Vaginal Tightening Gel? To empower women?? Really?!'

'So how tight is going to be right because a man's obviously got an ant in his pants?'

'This vaginal tightening gel may just sell. Because our society is not all well.'

Oh well.

Dettol

If mummies had a trusted partner in their role as the family's health guardians, it would not be the daddies. It would be Dettol.

Reckitt Benckiser's Dettol antiseptic liquid was launched in India (by the then Reckitt & Sons) way back in 1933. It found much use in hospitals because of its germicidal properties. Marketed to doctors and the health fraternity, it was one of the first products to rely on doctor referrals. Often recommended by the family's physician, over the years, it also found a place in the home. And became the object of a love-hate relationship with almost every middle-class Indian kid. Every time someone fell, cut their finger or bled in any way, out came the dreaded bottle of Dettol. It was basic first-aid, the antidote for every hurt other than a bleeding heart. The familiar, hospital-like smell made you shut your eyes tight as you waited for the dreaded, inevitable sting when Dettol was applied to an open cut or wound. Every middle-class mummy kept a bottle of Dettol in her arsenal. When her kids got hurt, she reassured them by applying Dettol on their wound, knowing that she had done what was necessary.

How does an iconic brand remain intact? How does it keep itself relevant to moms for so many decades, bridging the years and bridging generation gaps? What is the formula for its success?

It's quite simple, really. The Dettol promise of protection hinges on building awareness around the omnipotent, omnipresent, odourless, formless presence of GERMS. Mummies, beware.

Mothers see Dettol as an 'expert' – the ultimate and guaranteed protector from germs. Both Dettol and its consumers often compare the antiseptic liquid to a bodyguard, because it is a protector against the wildly unclean world outside the home.

Also seen as caring, Dettol has always been portrayed as a trusted champion of family health and, therefore, one of the brands that Indian mothers favour. No competitor has been able to usurp that position.

Dettol has some typical characteristics that have made it intrinsic to our psyche and our association to its germ-killing power – a characteristic smell, distinct clouding when put in water, and the *sting* (often more dreaded than the pain from the wound itself)! In fact, the unwelcome Dettol sting is so branded into our consciousness that consumers look for it in all antiseptic liquid brands. But no other brand stings quite the same. Strangely, some of the other liquids are seen as being not as effective as Dettol because they are gentler.

In an obvious reference to Dettol's dreaded sting, the Johnson & Johnson brand Savlon has tried to pitch itself as the antiseptic that doesn't hurt, though some say that is the very reason that Dettol's protection is trusted.

Savlon had ₹65 crore worth of sales in FY 2014, trailing Dettol. Till 2015, Dettol, with over 80 per cent market share (according to industry estimates), was the undisputed leader in the antiseptic liquid category in India worth ₹200 crore.[12]

But it has never been only about the sting. In its communication, Dettol has always played up its role of watchful protector. In a bit of clever symbology, it even uses the sword symbol in its packaging.

Over the years, the television commercials have at times emphasized that families which use Dettol regularly fall ill less often. Then, at times, they have talked of the uses Dettol can find in your home – from first-aid, to floor-mopping to bucket baths. For example, one of the earlier commercials showed how a baby could safely crawl on a floor that had been mopped with water to which Dettol antiseptic liquid had been added. And how a kid's injury could be cleaned with a similar solution. And how a child could spend a germy day out of the house but could still end up squeaky-clean after a bath with water to which the liquid had been added.

---

[12] 'How Savlon Could Soon be the New 'Dettol'', *Business Insider*, 31 August 2015

A recent commercial showed an expectant mother preparing for her baby's arrival with the help of Dettol antiseptic liquid. She is seen wiping down surfaces and washing the baby clothes with water to which the liquid has been added. In between, other Dettol products are strategically woven in. For instance, she makes her husband wash his hands with the brand's handwash and makes the parental figures sanitize their hands with the sanitizer. 'Dettol *se dhula*,' the ad tells you in the end.

And then, as always, it says, 'Be 100% sure,' which is the one thing loyalists have sworn by all these years.

Over time and through a variety of products, Dettol has tried to extend the umbrella of protection to other areas like soaps, hand sanitizers, shower gels, antibacterial wipes and liquid handwash as well. Major effort has been put into reminding consumers about the presence of germs in as many shocking ways as possible, including giving horns and evil eyes to the squiggly-wriggly computer-generated images of *keetanu*.

Often, the consumer is told some startling fact about germs. The delicious thing about these creatures is that they are omnipresent and invisible. A basic search will throw up all the ways they lurk waiting for us. For example, did you know that at this very moment the book you are reading has millions of germs on its cover? Or, is that a computer you are working on...did you know that the average computer keyboard has more germs than the potty seat in a loo? Are you off to wash your hands?

Take care. In case you weren't aware of it, the bar of soap you use is crawling with germs! Oh, and when you open the door to the loo, be careful because you do not know whether those who have used it before you washed their hands after peeing and before touching that door handle.

This is fantastic stuff. The knowledge of the presence of germs is what puts sanitizers and anti-bacterial handwashes (which are often from Dettol) on every household shopping list. Mummy has probably contributed to this by keeping Dettol antiseptic liquid at home. As far as she is concerned, Dettol is legend. (Though some ask that if Dettol does kill over 99 per cent of germs as it claims, isn't it that indestructible, leftover, minuscule percentage of germs that is actually legend?)

Whisper

'Fire at their balls,' the troops are rumoured to have screamed in the Finnish novel, *The Unknown Soldier*, as they charged at the enemy.

'I have the power,' roared the muscular hero of the *He Man* cartoon series as he rushed at the villain.

'Touch the pickle,' called out the girls in the Whisper sanitary napkin ad as they attacked, uh, the mango pickle.

As war cries go, the one with the pickle had a definite strangeness to it. But then, so did the taboos around menstruation that the slogan was battling.

For the longest time, the subject of women's periods was kept under wraps. We may have openly displayed our firearms but sanitary napkin purchases needed to be coyly and completely covered up before being handed over.

Considering the extent of mindspace that periods can take up in a woman's life, not to speak of the anxiety it can cause, Indian girls in sanitary napkin commercials were almost never shown raging or singing the blues. Actually, the only blue visible was the antiseptic sort of blue liquid being poured on to a futuristic-looking napkin. It was almost as if brands thought brave male viewers may get dizzy at the sight of blood.

'*Wo paanch din*' were sometimes acknowledged but the word 'menstruating' was almost never heard. And menopause seemed to strike women right after they finished with their twenties. How else would you explain the marked absence of older women in these ads?

These were all perfectly sterile and bashful ad scripts. And they presented an unexplored opportunity – for a brand to go brazenly where no pad had gone before – into a fully public airing of the *bleddy* business.

In the last century, advertising had already played a role in persuading consumers to feel a need that didn't exist before. In an area where homemade sanitary napkins had ruled the roost, 'hygiene', 'comfort' and 'health' were the key words advertising used to persuade women to adopt a readymade product.

From a simple pad in the early 1900s, the line-up had grown over the decades to include many innovations –

belted napkins, napkins with adhesive strips, napkins with gel-based padding and tampons being a few.

Quite a few brands were being discreetly peddled to women – Kotex, Whisper, Stayfree, Carefree, She Comfort, OB Tampons, Freshday. By 1990, it was clear that the sanitary napkin industry was all set to grow. All that was needed was the right strategy to reach the right section of consumers because, potentially, there were so many of them.

P&G launched Whisper in 1992. With its vast network in retail, there was immense opportunity for growth. By 2014, the product had proved quite popular and it was time to gather some emotional equity for the brand itself.

Whisper found that even Indian women from urban areas followed conventions inherited from an age-old time. These customs – mostly taboos – reflected the various do(n't)s and don'ts that were followed by women in different regions during their periods, because women were considered impure while menstruating and it was believed they would transfer their impurity to other things. (Just like a game of *dhappa*/tag, you are it!)

As a result, there were innumerable women who didn't water plants when they had their periods, didn't cut their nails, didn't wash their hair till the fifth day, didn't set curd and didn't go into the *puja* room (yes, even God wasn't safe in her 'polluting presence').

Though many women followed these practices, quite a few of them found them questionable. (There are, of course, naysayers who tell us that the practices evolved so that women could take a break from their chores, but that is not what this story is about.)

Of all these 'don'ts', there was one that seemed to be particularly peculiar – 'don't touch the pickle'. Many women would not touch, leave alone take out, pickle from a jar when menstruating. It was a popular, though incomprehensible, taboo. From it came the idea of telling girls to go ahead and 'touch the pickle'. The phrase rolled off the tongue, had a light-hearted call-to-revolution feel to it and was quirky enough to be memorable.

And so in 2014 came an ad film from Whisper that tried rallying all women. 'Touch the pickle' was the war cry.

The television commercial opened on a teenager touching that beige-ish *achaar ki burnee* you see in many kitchens, saying, 'touched the pickle jar.' Other women applauded. Meanwhile, the voiceover told girls to go ahead and 'touch the pickle' to rid themselves of taboos. The effort was to ensure that the 'touch the pickle' campaign would lead to discussions being held in public.

And it did. Shows on radio channels discussed period taboos, influencers on social media posted about it and there were debates on the topic on television channels. Apart from television, the ad saw a lot of exposure on digital media as well.

The brand was on the ball at all times. Sometimes, air time for the television commercial would be bought on receiving information that the subject of menstruation would be up for discussion at a particular time slot. Or, if something related to the topic came up on social media, Whisper would help it go viral while pushing their campaign.

For instance, at an event for Whisper, a journalist asked Bollywood actress Parineeti Chopra, a question in which he used the word 'problem' as a euphemism for 'period'. She pounced on this and pointed out how using the word should be as natural as a girl having her period. Whisper picked this up and made it a topic of discussion because it was so relevant to the campaign.

Front-page ads were placed in leading newspapers across major cities. People were invited to participate in the buzz around the subject. There were photo ops and events for the campaign. Women stepped forward to tell their 'taboo stories', anthropologists talked about the backgrounds of these taboos and innovative pull-outs were inserted into magazines.

Menstrupedia's founder Aditi Gupta gave a TED talk on the matter. Stars like Kalki Koechlin, Mandira Bedi, Tanvi Azmi and Shraddha Kapoor; medical expert, Dr Suneela Garg; women achievers like India's first female surfer, Ishita Malviya, and the first twins to scale Mt Everest – Nungshi and Tashi – were all seen talking about these irrational taboos.

A nationwide movement of sorts was the aim, with television, public relations and digital support. What worked was that the communication showed girls doing everything that they are not 'supposed' to do during their periods – wearing white, touching pickle and playing sports.

The campaign received exposure across media and caught the attention of the BBC, *Financial Times*, *Reuters* and the *Wall Street Journal*. To top it all, it won the Glass Lion Grand Prix at the Cannes International Festival of Creativity, which recognizes work that addresses gender inequality or prejudice through the conscious representation of gender in advertising.

Most significantly, though, the campaign encouraged women, young and old, to talk openly about menstruation.

Since then, many actors have started endorsing sanitary napkins. Brands like Sofy and Stayfree joined in the conversation with digital campaigns.

But it was Whisper whose share of voice grew from 21 per cent to 91 per cent.[13] The brand made it its purpose to advocate for women and empower them. To that end, it pledged to educate 15 million girls on menstrual hygiene in the following years.[14]

Continuing to be pretty much the leader in the sanitary napkin market, Whisper showed it's sometimes good to say, let's talk, period. While 'to bleed or not to bleed' had never been the question, Whisper helped push menstrual conversation out of its existential crisis.

---

[13] Sachs, MaryLee, 'Glass Lion Educates Marketers', *Forbes*, 7 July 2015

[14] http://www.exchange4media.com/events/iprcca-2016/casestudy/campaign-104.aspx

It's probably just a matter of time before someone notices those signs outside some places of worship that go, 'For the sake of our holiness, it is requested that menstruating women do not enter. Thank you for understanding.'

Titan Raga

Many years ago, Raga did not remind us of funny memes about a political figure. Raga was simply a range of watches from Titan, designed exclusively for women.

In marketing, as in politics, many a thought has been adopted and discarded in the *aaya-raam-gaya-raam* spirit of the game. Over the years, Raga too has seen a change in what its ads portray.

Raga was launched in 1992 and was introduced as a range specifically designed for women. At that time, women were often simply offered 'For Her' versions of male watches. Raga was different. In keeping with its name, the watch had a uniquely Indian identity.

The brand started out by being a decorative watch that women could use as an accessory, like an essential piece of jewellery with which they could also tell time.

Even in 2007, it was portrayed very clearly as a replacement for jewellery. An ad starring Rani Mukherji, released in 2007, showed her putting aside the flower from her hair, her earrings, her bracelet, her anklets and choosing a watch from her jewellery box. It was, of course, a Titan Raga giving her *ek khoobsoorat saath*. (To the all-too-familiar signature tune of Titan ads which was actually from Mozart's '25th Symphony'. But we digress.)

Fast forward to 2014. Titan had a marketshare of over 40 per cent in the ₹5,300-crore Indian watch market and was selling some 16 million pieces every year.[15] By this time, with the changing times, women's empowerment was a catchphrase and a tune, the marketers at Titan realized, that was perfect for their Raga.

Raga aired a film in 2014 which showed an elegant woman (the very elegantly put-together Nimrat Kaur) accidentally meeting an old acquaintance at an airport. They greet each other warmly and sit down to catch up. Very soon, you realized he is an ex-boyfriend, an old flame.

As they exchange notes, a wistful tone of what-might-have-been creeps into the guy's conversation.

Gradually, there comes a point during which the girl (and the audience) realize that he thought it was because of her that their relationship could not go further, because she didn't want to quit her job like he wanted her to. *Ugh*. She touches the Raga as if to emphasize the watch on her wrist and goes on to say that he clearly hadn't changed (as far as his plainly regressive views went). And, of course, she offers him a coffee. '*Khud se naya rishta*', Titan Raga tells you.

---

[15] Shashidhar, Ajita, 'Makeover Time', *Business Today*, 28 September 2014

Affirmation came quickly. The ad was viewed over 1.4 lakh times on YouTube[16] within a week of being uploaded.

Titan's portrayal of an empowered, self-assured woman, who was comfortable with her choices and knew her mind, struck a chord. It was a departure from the norm but much in keeping with the prevailing sentiment.

This showed in the outpouring of response on social media towards the brand, which had taken a stand so subtly and effectively.

And it also showed in all the jeers on social media for the Male Chauvinist Pappu, who obviously hadn't passed muster.

To conclude what is evident is sometimes the person portrayed in an ad is someone the target audience may identify with or even aspire to be. And while times and roles may keep evolving, some things remain the same. Like *maa ka karz*, which can never be repaid. It can only be passed on. In general, the doling out of *karz* is in the form of *doodh*/Bournvita. But sometimes, Moms also loan emotional moments like – Vicks Vaporub-bing to clear noses or by making *maa ki daal*.

But it must have been a sign of the times when, finally, the woman in an ad sipped her Women's Horlicks and told you the reason why, 'Because your body needs you, too.'

---

[16] Sen, Sohini, 'Titan Raga: For the Elegant, Evolved Woman', *afaqs!*, 16 December 2014

Kids are a whole lot more than cute props in ads or ignorant consumers now. The kiddie grapevine has it that a place in Pune has big boys devising the crafty little Kinderjoy toys, which are then sent for approval – to no less an authority than school kids themselves.

Men on motorcycles are known to be thundering their way home for Diwali and Coca-Cola. Meanwhile, some men like smelling 'mantastic' with Old Spice.

And then, at times, there comes a campaign like 'Bold is beautiful' from Anouk clothing which, unconventionally, touches on lesbianism.

Advertising mirrors. And it summarizes, in thirty seconds, imagery that has been decades in the making – like dishwashing husbands, mommy brides and bossy babies. Oh, and noodle-strap blouses too.

BTM

BRANDJIS TURNED MODERN

Boy-talk, being the reliable barometer that it is, tells us that for many men the ideal woman is she who they can take home to meet Mummy over chai, who will help Mummy make the chai maybe even *pakodas*; but who will also banter with the gang at Happy Hours, go for the *golgappa* vodka shots and laugh at your joke about how the Playboy founder reached heaven via-Agra.

Hmm, could it be that these boys are all looking for personalized BTMs – that all-encompassing, if condescending, campus phrase that refers to *Behenjis* Turned *Mod*. (Of course, there is a *Bhaiyyaji* Turned *Mod* version too but we digress.)

To stretch the analogy, it stands to reason that if we like traditional-modern individuals, we may just like our products to be that way too. *Mod* being a subset of 'Westernized,' we do have many Brands Turned *Mod* with traditional-modern offerings – *Dosa* chips in cheese flavour, anyone?

Successful marketers have the ability to 'adjust' to our preferences. They know we like tomato sauce as much as the next American but they also know we like it with some *desi* soul (that is *mirchi* please). And they know that their cars may be marvels of technology but we have an obssession with *petrole* consumption.

But they also know how not to mess with some legacies. If we believe that, for the last hundred years or so, film stars have looked good because of one brand of soap, well, so be it. Why fix what's not broken?

Yes, in some of our most iconic ad campaigns, the insights are quite universal (the universe being India). Know your consumer, said an ad guru. Especially the Indian consumer, he could have added. Because in this country, we like our Brands Turned *Mod* our way.

Bingo!

Just when you thought the marketing of Indian munchies was at its most *jhakaas*, someone came along and made it kick*aas*. This happened around the time that *bindaas* – which used to be a state of mind – became available as the flavour of a snack from ITC.

In 2007, the fast-moving branded snacks market was worth about ₹2,000 crore, growing at 30 per cent per year. Around this time, ITC Ltd, a conglomerate that already had its finger in many pies, decided to get into the snacks segment. The only big competitor they had to counter at this time was PepsiCo's Frito Lay, with its hugely popular range of brands like Lay's, Cheetos, Kurkure and Uncle Chipps.[1]

Before entering the segment, ITC decided to do its homework and launched a massive research project. For months, a team of people appointed by the company travelled around the country exploring regional snacks. Their task was to find out everything there was to know about *khakras*, *golgappas*, *bhel-puris* and what have you. Seriously.

[1] 'Bingo! ITC Has Finally Got It', Rediff.com, 1 May 2007

(When did they interview for *that* job?)

The team also studied the consumer segments for these items and came back with tons of data and analysis about consumer preferences, habits and behaviour patterns with regard to snacking. ITC concluded that to make the most of their new brand of snacks, they would have to target people in the age group of 20 to 35.

It's not clear at which point of time during the analysis and decision-making ITC said, 'Bingo! That's it.' But, in all probability, it was around the time that all the data they had collected led to a single insight – that the majority of consumers liked the taste of homegrown snacks served up with a contemporary twist. Let it not be said that we Indians are not adventurous.

ITC proceeded to rope in chefs from their hotel chain to transform existing, popular snacks into something *thoda hatke*. Metaphorically, ITC played fairy godmother to our combined Cinderella lives and transformed our everyday *roti-kaddu* into snacks that were fit to be eaten at a royal ball. (Disclaimer: No *kaddu* actually goes into the making of the snacks.) The chefs magically created more than a dozen different flavours which were later given names like Bindaas, Masti Chhaas, Nimboo Achaar and Tandoori Tikka.

ITC then launched a brand called Bingo! as a ready-to-eat range of packaged snacks in 2007. Today, the range includes variants of potato chips and finger snacks.

One of the products under the Bingo! brand was Mad Angles. This hybrid chip, neither a nacho nor exactly a *khakhra*, could boast of something that no other snack in the market had – a triangular shape. The focus of the marketing for Mad Angles was to establish its name and ensure recognition and recall. Its unique shape (and exciting new flavours) provided just the right ingredient.

All this novelty was reflected in the ads too.

The ad film for Mad Angles Achari Masti opened on a discussion in a boardroom, where respectable-looking corporate executives were trying to decide on the best shape for the snack from three different options – the options themselves being three identical triangles. After a typical round of bored-room discussion, the film ended with 'Mad Angles Achari Masti. *Har* angle *se mmmm...*'

People liked the nonsensical ad, and they loved the flavours and the texture of the snack itself. The brand was on its way to recording quite a success story.

Humour was part of the communication for other Bingo! products as well. One film for potato chips showed a whole lot of pink flamingos crowding the screen. Even as you focused on one bird, an expressionless voiceover talked about the birds and their characteristics, how they did have long beaks to help them find food (here the expressionless voice became animated) but could not have the delicious combination of tandoori paneer tikka and potato chips – a combination offered by Bingo!. In the closing frame, along with a pack of Bingo! came the descriptor: 'Bingo! No confusion. Great combination.'

Another ad had a CBI inspector clarifying the difference between a criminal called Zango and Bingo!'s potato wafers, trying to build better brand recall with interplay between similar-sounding words.

To ensure reach for the ads, ITC created and promoted a website dedicated to the brand showcasing offers, freebies, downloads and games. The television commercials were aired mostly on channels that catered to the youth, like MTV and Star World, news channels and popular Hindi channels like Zee and Star TV. On the radio, Bingo! spots were heard in the time slots during which consumers were commuting to or from work. Apart from print ads in leading national dailies, multiple hoardings also displayed the product.

The Indian flavours and ITC's distribution network ensured trials and Bingo! became an important brand for ITC. So while PepsiCo still dominated the chips market, Bingo! Mad Angles was made a star debut and created its very own niche.

In the end, most people agreed that while Mad Angles were great, the ad angles were pretty good too.

Maruti Suzuki

Once upon a time, if your heart beat faster for a certain Padmini, you needed to scold it by telling it to be still, because chances were that you would have to wait for ten years to get near her.

Premier Padmini was the car that was licensed from Fiat and launched in India in 1973. Buying one was not for the impatient, and if you were fortunate enough to get yours, you might have preferred to drive it around a bit and sell it because its resale price was sometimes higher than its showroom price! At the time, apart from the Padmini, there were only a few brands you could aspire to – Hindustan Motors' Ambassador and the Herald from Standard Motor Products.

Then the 1980s arrived and along came Maruti Suzuki with its '800' and everything changed. Maruti Suzuki, incorporated as Maruti Udyog Limited (MUL) in 1981, was a joint venture of the Indian government and the Suzuki Motor Corporation of Japan. The first Maruti 800 car rolled out in 1983. The Maruti Omni and Gypsy soon followed.

The Maruti 800 was smaller and more delicate than the cars that Indian consumers were used to (some fuss-pots even called it 'tinny'), but was considered to be great value-for-money. People would book a Maruti 800 and then make money on their purchase by selling the allotment papers to those who didn't want to wait. As time went on, though, the waiting periods became shorter.

The brand marked a turning point for the Indian automobile sector. In 1970, the total number of passenger vehicles sold annually was 32,000. Come 2016, this figure had increased to 20,00,000.[2] Contributing to this increase was the fact that multiple brands had made forceful appearances on the automobile scene and the types of vehicles and demand for them across segments – minis, SUVs, luxury sedans, what have you – had gone through the (sun)-roof.

Which is why it seemed for a while there that Maruti Suzuki would face big challenges in maintaining its share of the market. Yet, Maruti Suzuki continues to be a name to be reckoned with, still recording high growth and sales year on year. This success can partly be attributed to the clever marketing strategies and memorable ads that emerged from Maruti's stables.

Today, the target audience for Maruti Suzuki is a mixed lot, though first-time buyers still make up a huge chunk. The first-time buyer is a person who does many rounds of research, scours the Internet and takes feedback from Chintu *ke chacha* and *pados ke* Mehta*ji*. Selling to him needs a deep insight into his psyche.

Some car owners want an additional car or are replacing the home's second car. Sometimes the buyer is not the user, and the car is bought for a young person. In any of these scenarios, apart from the purchase price, an important consideration is the cost of maintaining the vehicle on the road. Whatever the factors that come into play, the common concern among car buyers

---

[2] Baggonkar, Swaraj, '40 Years Ago...and Now: From 32,000 Cars a Year to 2.5 Million', *Business Standard*, 25 January 2015

across the country, a national obsession almost, is a car's mileage.

In a country where fuel prices have always been a cause for alarm, a large percentage of car buyers are known to reject a car of choice in favour of a car that delivers on mileage. Many of them may be interested in new launches, but they end up buying something that is known to be fuel-savvy. A car's mileage is a key topic of conversation among car owners and may incite pride, envy, disappointment or smug satisfaction, as the situation warrants. And it is always a matter of curiosity. In its communication, it is this subject of mileage that Maruti Suzuki tackled in quirky, memorable ways.

In 2010, a television commercial for the brand opened on a serious-looking, I'm-from-NASA-type scientist droning on in a practised way, describing a hi-tech spacecraft to a group of Indian tourists, who look impassive. Even as he is seen describing some uber-cool detail pertaining to the spacecraft, one unimpressed Indian asks, '*Kitna deti hai?*' The film ends with a voiceover that says, 'For a country obsessed with mileage, Maruti Suzuki makes India's most fuel-efficient cars', followed by: 'Maruti Suzuki. A way of life.'

The follow-up campaign that came in 2012, portrayed some more unexpected and unlikely situations ending with the inevitable query, '*Kitna deti hai?*' One such commercial, set sometime in the 1930s, opened on a woman aviator, Amelia Johnson. A pioneering long-distance, solo flier of sorts, it showed her landing in Mumbai and holding a press conference. As she talks about exciting things like horsepower, the radial engine and the thousand-mile range of her aircraft, someone from the audience interrupts her to ask, *'Kitna deti hai?'* followed, again, by the Maruit Suzuki voiceover, promoting its fuel-efficient cars.

Another film opened underwater. Two scuba divers happen to come across a man on an underwater bike. In sign language, they admire the bike and are told about its cool features, which include its being able to move at 20 knots. Uninspired, one of the divers asks the biker, *'Kitna deti hai?'*

The memorable campaign delivered on raising the perception of the brand's commitment to fuel-efficiency. And since this was so important in the Indian context, it reaffirmed that Maruti Suzuki was a name to trust. By 2016–2017, even with much competition all around, Maruti's market share was around 47.45 per cent, and with an annual capacity sales of 1.442 million units it held on to the distinction of being India's largest car maker.[3]

Paper Boat

For a certain generation, tearing a page out of a book and making paper boats is inextricably linked to *bachpan ki yaadein*. So when a brand tears a page out

[3] Mukherjee, Sharmistha, '40 Years Ago...and Now: How the People's Car Was Born and How it Stayed That Way', *Business Standard*, 19 November 2014

of that book, calls itself Paper Boat and offers you packs upon packs of chilled drinks, brimming with flavours from the days gone by – *aam panna*, *kalakhatta* and *paani puri* to name just a few – it's like getting a *tatkal* passport to childhood.

Through the late 2000s, the energy drink market was growing in India and, not surprisingly, many people wanted a serving. Among them was an energy drink going by the zany name of Tzinga. It was launched in 2011 in Delhi and Bengaluru. The parent company, Hector Beverages, with an eye on the gigantic market that had been cornered by the Austrian energy drink Red Bull, had priced Tzinga at ₹20, a lot lower than Red Bull.

The strategy worked, but only for a while. Soon, distribution costs began to pinch the company, and it did not help that Tzinga had very few variants that could boost their revenues. The founders of Hector Beverages, therefore, decided to look into product options. The story goes that the founders were one day discussing the delightful *aam panna* made by one of their mothers, when suddenly, just like that, they hit upon a delicious new idea – a range of drinks that brought to people familiar, regional flavours that would probably not be available far away from their homes. They decided to name the brand, Paper Boat, which itself evoked nostalgia.

The Paper Boat way of communicating their brand proposition to the consumer was to focus on 'drinks and memories', to hark back to how a particular flavour was prepared and consumed maybe even a century ago, and note the ingredients and recipes and the different forms they took. The effort was always to keep it simple and familiar. Aam Panna and Jaljeera, both flavours from grandmothers' and mothers' kitchens, were the first two Paper Boat flavours launched in August 2013. Over the next couple of years came others – Golgappe ka Pani, Kalakhatta, Aamras, Thandai, Anar and Kokum. Each type was instantly reminiscent of a taste, a smell and a time long ago. Even though the supermarket shelves showcased the range without *baarish ka paani* or a storytelling *nani*, nostalgia communicated simply through the names of the drinks compelled shoppers to check out the packs.

One kind of consumer was the experimental kind, who would try a new flavour in the market because, well, it was new – and would come back for more because she or he loved the taste.

The other kind was the one who responded to the nostalgia plank. These customers held on to their memories of homemade childhood drinks but often had no access to them and were drawn to traditional flavours made available in a shop.

The brand decided to focus single-mindedly on memories. The plan was to begin with the major cities – Delhi, Mumbai and Bengaluru – which has large migrant populations who hankered for a taste of home.

In 2015, the company orchestrated the recreation of childhood memories in a film over three minutes long.

The fact that the film was narrated by Gulzar and had the track from the *Malgudi Days* TV serial of the

1980s helped in recreating the magic and joy of childhood experiences. It began in a very familiar way. A boy tears a page out of his school notebook to make a paper boat much as we all have done as children. He launches the boat into a stream and so begins a journey into childhood memories – walking with friends from school while a bullock cart carried schoolbags and water bottles; leaping on to a pile of clothes on a bed, telling grandpa a story, making a touch-me-not leaf shut by touching it, sniffing at a freshly erased page, smearing one's face with Holi colours, running to grab a kite the string of which has been cut, standing open-mouthed in the rain to catch the fat drops, pouncing on and cuddling up with grandma, getting the antenna on the roof in position so you could watch *Vikram-Vetaal* on Doordarshan, counting out coins to buy something from a shop's candy jars, deciding on getting an injection on the arm instead of the butt, feeding a mailbox a letter, feeding a puppy, refusing the height-increasing plank placed on the chair at the barber's and choosing to sit normally, being made to climb through the ventilator to open a door latched from the inside...

The film ends with a young man drinking from a Paper Boat pack. The voiceover tells you, '*Bachpan ki yaadon ko fir se bahao, badi chatpati hai yeh fir se pilao,*' reinforcing that the brand was about 'drinks and memories'.

While the target audience was urban professionals in their twenties and early thirties, the ad was made to appeal to just about anyone. There were also commercials focused on a specific product. The stories they told were about the growing-up years and their association with a sense of wonder at the world, of curiosity and exploration and the small things that make childhood years so magical.

For example, there was the young man sitting in an aircraft with Paper Boat Aamras. He takes a swig from the pack and is transported to the time when his Dad showed him how to squeeze a mango so that when he bit into the skin, he could almost drink the pulp.

Another film showed a little girl stealing the ruby-red pomegranate seeds her mother is extracting. Her hand is slapped away but she cannot resist making off with the bowl full of seeds even as her mother smiles indulgently. The film ends with the girl, now a young woman, remembering this with a smile as she drains a Paper Boat *anaar* pack.

Media vehicles, whether print, outdoor or television, were used with specific objectives. The television commercials bolstered the Paper Boat multimedia campaign and remained the medium that the media budget led with, but digital marketing was crucial to the plot too. Year-long digital programmes and activity on social media platforms, including Instagram campaigns, were planned.

The packaging of the drinks too helped to create appeal. Not only were the soft, squishy packs easy to carry, but the subtle graphics and design also added to their attractiveness, not to mention the theme of memories. Initially, the company had a plant in Manesar in Haryana churning out packs. Later, they added a plant in Mysore with an even larger manufacturing capacity to help meet the increasing demand. This simultaneously served to consolidate the brand's presence in the west and the south.

Paper Boat's range of 'fortified, functional and non-carbonated beverages', was at ₹72 crore in 2015–16 from ₹32 crores the previous year.[4]

The proof of the success of their concept – ethnic/ Indian beverages – is evident in the me-toos that have sprung up since their inception. Apart from smaller companies in the unorganized sector, the very respectable, very large Dabur has a similar range of drinks that they have branded Hajmola Yoodley.

Who would have thought that Paper Boat would be the face that launched a thousand sips?

Lux

K*kkkkkkkya*?!

Had dream-boy Shah Rukh Khan become one of the girls? There he sat, prettily naked, in a bathtub. (You assumed he was naked because, well, he was in a bathtub after all. And because there were rose petals strewn cunningly across the water to hide everyone-

[4] Maheshwari, Richa, 'Paper Boat Has Wind in its Sails, But Losses Rise', *Economic Times*, 15 December 2016

knows-what.) Meanwhile, around the tub posed some pretty august company – Hema Malini, Juhi Chawla, Kareena Kapoor and Sridevi. His endorsement was quite ladylike too: '*Aaj mein aap ko batanewala hoon meri khubsoorati ka raaz* – Lux.'

No! Really? Was Bollywood's *baadshah* actually posing in a Lux ad – a preserve exclusive to women?

The year was 2005, the 75th anniversary of Lux, HUL's iconic soap brand, and a very special ad was needed. The strategy was to retain the hallmarks of a typical Lux ad *but* to play on it and make it worthy of a product that has been dominant in its product category for 75 years.

Right through its long history, the brand had been consistent in its communication. As a classic example of a successful celebrity-endorsed product, there are many things that make up the Lux formula. Though film stars have been the keystone in Lux's communication, the ads have always talked about the brand, not about the stars. The bottom line has always been that of beauty, glamour and luxury.

Lux's tryst with beauty in India began years ago, in 1929 when it was launched in India as the beauty soap of film stars. Since then, many brands tried using stars to announce their arrival but if there was one brand that certified that a star had arrived, it was Lux. Featuring in a Lux ad was almost a rite of passage to stardom.

So how did Lux hold on to its iconic status over the years?

When Lux was launched in India, it was the first mass-market luxury soap around. Instead of taking the personal hygiene route, Lux chose beauty – not beauty of the indefinable kind but the very obvious, in-your-face-beauty of film stars. It was a route that the brand worked on successfully for over seventy years

In the beginning, the ads showed foreign film stars. It was only in 1941 that Lux used the svelte, popular Indian film star Leela Chitnis, as its first Indian model. The copy in the ad could not be clearer in its promise – 'Your skin will be fresh and smooth'. The messaging highlighted just one thing – Leela Chitnis' beauty existed because she bathed with Lux.

Since then Lux packaged itself as the stars' solution for great skin. The celebrity ads, besides being memorable, worked in assuring people of quality. In fact, quality and price featured high in the brand's recall. If beauty, fragrance, lather and quality were what consumers were looking for in a premium luxury soap, then Lux identified and showcased these elements quite perfectly.

So when Lux's 75th anniversary came around in India, the question was – how would you make an anniversary ad that was different yet stuck to the brand attributes?

Well, to the line of superstars who have sworn allegiance to the brand, you simply add a megastar with a difference (this time in gender) who will not only grab eyeballs but reinforce the brand's premium stature.

And so, across India, four new variants of Lux in distinct 75th-year celebratory packs, were endorsed by queens of Bollywood like Hema Malini, Juhi Chawla, Kareena Kapoor and Sridevi. And the King himself, Shah Rukh Khan.

So as he sat in the exclusive ladies tub, surrounded by these legendary screen queens, they talked of the 75th-anniversary Lux pack-wrappers, some of which would win some lucky people a whole year's supply of Lux. Then SRK went on to say that since the company needed a superstar for this occasion, he told them '*Main hoon na*'. (At which point the Hema-Juhi-Kareena-Sridevi quartet dunk his head under water and leave him to his bath.)

Even with the tongue-in-cheek reference to his appearance in the ad, Shah Rukh Khan became the latest entry to an exclusive ladies' club, the first male superstar bold enough to appear in a Lux ad in India.

And if you're known by the company you keep, then, Shah Rukh *baba* joined the League of Lux ladies, which had as its members Madhuri Dixit, Aishwarya Rai, Karishma Kapoor, Priyanka Chopra, Katrina Kaif, Mahima Choudhry, Madhubala, Nargis, Meena Kumari, Mala Sinha, Sharmila Tagore, Waheeda Rehman, Saira Banu, Hema Malini and Zeenat Aman to name just a few. (And in her day, the late 'Amma' or erstwhile All India Anna Dravida Munnetra Kazhagam chief, Jayalalithaa, too had modelled for Lux.)

In the last century, toilet soaps had become an increasingly crowded category. One of the most trusted brands in India, Lux held its own by introducing premium yet affordable variants. While the film star factor remained constant (the brand also sponsored many events like the Lux Zee Cine awards, emphasizing this association), Lux also consistently evolved in its packaging and in its offerings, extending into a range of shower gels, liquid soaps and moisturizing bars to retain the loyalty of the customers when strong rivals arrived on the scene. The brand maintained its status because of factors that have always worked for it. It even kept milk-cream as a key ingredient in variants because it evoked the desired imagery for the brand.

The fact that HUL was the parent company ensured Lux had access to a formidable supply and distribution network. So, though Lux faced pressure in an extremely competitive segment, it also possessed a very strong brand image in the market, especially in the beauty segment. And it had a starry association that showed no sign of losing its lustre. Not even when they put Shah Rukh in hot water, raising many an eyebrow.

But in the process, also scoring a *kkkk*coup of sorts.

Star Sports

'Cricket is a game played by asses and watched by the masses,' said someone brave once.

Yes, brave, because in India saying such things is sacrilege, and tantamount to treason. In recent times, the cricket-watching masses have also increased dramatically in number with platforms across media delivering easy-to-consume cricket content in newer formats – the heavily promoted, mega-marketed one-dayers and T20s. (Yes, bring on the green hair, the quickie versions and, of course, the cheerleaders!)

Way back, in 1983, millions of Indians followed the World Cup, then known as the Prudential Cup and now as the ICC Cricket World Cup, on newly acquired television sets. When India won the World Cup and Kapil Dev scored immortality, the country frenzied itself into an obsession with cricket in general and the World Cup in particular.

Ever since then, for any television channel, cricket is perceived as *the* hot seller. Getting the rights to broadcast a cricketing property is a sure-fire way of attracting viewers. Having cricket in the arsenal takes care of more than just the cricketing programming, since the sport ensures profitability even when the rest of the channel's content is not as sticky for audiences.

This is especially true for the ICC Cricket World Cup – that lung-busting, passion-inducing war that comes around once in four years. Needless to say, channels compete intensely to be part of that jingoism.

In 1983, most Indians had watched the World Cup on good old Doordarshan, the sole broadcaster in those days. Over the years, a number of sports channels entered the scene – Star, Zee, Neo Sports, Neo Prime, Six and DD Sports, all jostling for the consumers' attention.

When the 2015 World Cup came around, Star Sports wanted to maximize on the opportunity. The focus was on achieving as high a viewership across the country as possible, and when it was announced that India's first match would be played against Pakistan, it was time to go all out.

To begin with, they packed the commentary box till it was bursting with sports stars. There was Wasim Akram, Allan Border, Kapil Dev, Ian Botham, Sunil Gavaskar, Mark Waugh, Shane Warne, Graeme Smith, Rahul Dravid, Saurav Ganguly, to name a few. The plan was to supply viewers with ball-by-ball data from matches past and present and have analytics that spanned thousands of match-hours. There was also going to be live streaming on their website and the offer of 24-hour access to on-demand videos through web, WAP and apps.[5]

There was technology, of course, to bring the viewer as close to the game as possible. With drone cameras, Star wanted to provide an eye-in-the-sky experience. The arsenal was in place and it was now time to bring in the viewership.

India were the defending champions. The strategy for the marketing campaign was clear: to whip up the country's loyalty and make Indians root for their team to win the World Cup all over again.

There was one particular angle that Star Sports wanted to explore. India's opening match was one that was guaranteed to set pulses racing and eyeballs popping –

[5] 'Star Sports Shouts #WeWon'tGiveItBack for ICC Cricket World Cup 2015', *afaqs!*, 30 January 2015

India was going to battle Pakistan. The point was to take advantage of all the excitement and create communication tailored to this specific clash.

The overall launch campaign was based on a simple thought, 'We won't give it back.' This was about a determined and aggressive Team India which had the crown and there was no way they were about to give it up. The ad around India vs Pakistan was a subset of this and planned along playful lines.

In the hugely exciting matter of India's opening match, there was scope for much fun, ribbing and *nok-jhok*. It just so happened that Pakistan had never yet won a match against India in a World Cup scenario.

Never.

So what did Pakistanis feel about this? What could be the Pakistani cricket supporter's point of view? Enter, the Pakistani fan – the one whose desire for that victory was greater than anyone else's. His perspective was tinged with pain and longing of the dramatically intense kind. Such pain needed to be exploited! On behalf of all of India, twist the knife where it hurt. *Umm*, sportingly, of course.

In a unique twist, Star Sports's communication looked at the scenario from the rival's side. In the television commercial that Star Sports created for India's opening match against Pakistan, a Pakistani cricket fan is shown looking for an opportunity – a *mauka* – of celebrating India's defeat. This match provided that *mauka*, when his team could win and he got to bust out the balloons (or actually the firecrackers, which is what the entire subcontinent was known to do). The Pakistani fan is seen with a box of fireworks kept aside, all set to celebrate the moment in which his team defeated the Indian team. This is in 1992. From then till 2011, he is shown waiting for the win. He gets older, his television sets change, he even acquires a family – all the while waiting for that *mauka*, that all-important defeat of India by Pakistan. All this to the unlikely war cry of '*Mauka, mauka!*' chanted *qawaali*-style.

As almost never happens, this subset ad staged an upset. The ad proved to be so overwhelmingly popular that Star Sports decided on taking the thought forward into every match. The communication for the India–Pakistan match, especially the '*mauka, mauka*' chant became the rallying point for the entire campaign. India won its match against Pakistan, but the films kept coming. They now showed the Pakistani *Mauka* Man still waiting, now to celebrate India's defeat – at the hands of any team!

The India–Pakistan enmity on the cricket field has always been the stuff folklore is made of. Its rendering in a teasing, humorous, tongue-in-cheek manner was just what the audiences ordered. As a whole, the campaign saw the human and emotional element of cricket being emphasized. For once, it was not just about the gods of cricket but about the dreams and ambitions – and the little rituals and rites of passage – of devoted fans.

What started as a one-off film became the pilot of a mini-series of sorts. The first ad was released on YouTube and this helped in creating a buzz around the words '*mauka, mauka*'. Once the films were aired on television, the buzz snowballed gigantically. Within half a day of going online, the first *mauka* ad organically garnered over a million views. Overall, the ads got more than 30 million views – among the most during the World Cup.[6]

Milking the unforeseen response, Star Sports started creating two films a week on an average. After every match, their marketing, creative, programming and social media specialists would work out the context of the *Mauka* Man's next appearance. Television Viewer Ratings for the India versus Pakistan match shot up. Today, '*mauka, mauka*' remains a very dominant ad memory from that particular World Cup.

India did not win the World Cup, but it was only when the Indian team exited from the World Cup that the cross-border reach of the *Mauka* Man was highlighted. At that time, apparently, Pakistani fans got their own back by making calls to the headquarters of the Board of Cricket Control in India (BCCI) and chanting – you guessed it – '*mauka, mauka!*'

Tata Tea

In popular media, tea has typically been portrayed as the drink that makes India feel alert, integrates new *bahus*

[6] Amsan, Andrew, 'The Story Behind the "Mauka" Campaign', *Sunday Guardian*, 28 March 2015

into households and welcomes guests into a home. But tea as a champion for social causes? Who would have thought of that? Well, Tata Global Beverages did – and made many of us warm up to the idea.

Many brands of tea have competed to be our daily cuppa over the years. Tata Global Beverages has Tata Tea and Tetley. Then there's Wagh Bakri, Godrej, Society, Duncan and Lipton to name a few. And there is the heritage brand, Brooke Bond, which is over 140 years old and going strong as one of the largest tea brands of Hindustan Unilever Limited.

Adding to the boil in large and middle-sized cities across India, tea was increasingly being pitted against coffee and the coffee-shop culture. There was a perception of coffee being trendy and aspirational while tea had acquired a bit of a fuddy-duddy aura.

By the early 2000s, there were so many factors at play that Tata Tea needed something special to stand out. The Tata Tea brands – Premium, Gold, Agni and Life – each had different marketing campaigns. An umbrella campaign with a binding thought would not only strengthen brand image, it would also help Tata Tea get more for their money.

They hit upon a brilliant insight: The growing sense of frustration among the youth that few brands had addressed. By creating a platform for social activism, Tata Tea had the chance to be perceived as a partner, and tea had a chance to become youthful and a young person's drink.

Tata Tea's campaign in 2007 had exactly that as its call to action: '*Roz subah sirf utho nahi. Jaago Re.*' It was a call for social awakening. One of the first television commercials they released with this message at its core picked up on the familiar scenario of a politician visiting a neighbourhood, asking for votes. A young man was shown turning the tables on him by asking him about the qualifications and achievements he possessed, which made him worthy of the 'big job' of running the nation. The ad conveyed a powerful message. It told the nation to wake up, to act, just like the young tea-drinking man.

As a thought, this hit the spot.

From 2008 onwards, Tata Tea geared its campaign towards mobilizing young people to vote in the forthcoming elections. Their message: Just holding the government accountable for things that went wrong was not all right if people did not take responsibility themselves. If nothing else, every individual needed to turn up and vote on voting day so that no vote would go to waste and each person could be a part of the politics of the country.

Tata Tea spread the word with its commercials and collaterals and also worked on a mobile campaign. Striking a chord with the youth during the 2009 elections, the campaign reached out to the massive voter base – many of whom were eighteen years old and above. These were people eligible to vote and definitely old enough to drink tea. A website they created – www.jaagore.com – educated first-time voters about the voting process.

One of the ads shows a man holding a flask of tea, standing in front of a cinema hall. He keeps offering tea to anyone passing by saying, '*Aap so kyon rahe hain?* Chai *peejiye.*' People stare at him as if he's gone mad. Finally, a woman tells him irritably that she is not sleeping; it is a holiday and she is there to watch a movie. He looks at her and says emphatically, 'Election. *Agar aap vote nahin dengi, toh aap so rahee hain.*' He then says, 'Voting *ke liye* register *karein*, jaagore.com.' The commercial ends on the message, '*Agar aap sote rahe to yeh desh kaise jaagega?*'

The website got over 28 lakh registrations and more than a fourth of those who registered did vote.[7]

The response to the campaign was tremendously positive – so much so that Tata Tea decided to get bolder on '*Jaago Re*'. Over the years, the brand began addressing many relevant social issues, including those related to gender. In each step, whether it was print, television, radio or online, Tata Tea went all out. In places that did not have access to their communication, they often sent out volunteers to spread the word.

In 2009, a disillusioned country warmed up to a newer set of ads that raised awareness about corruption. During the anti-corruption movement led by Anna Hazare, Tata Tea ran a campaign with the message, '*Aaj se khilana bandh, pilana shuru*', which got a couple of lakh people vowing to never give bribes.

7 'Tata Tea Launches New "Jaago Re" Campaign, on Corruption', *Business Standard*, 20 January 2013

As a platform, Tata Tea's *Jaago Re* proved to be both – multifaceted and long-lasting. Nothing like a good tea party to kick off a revolution with.

Fair and Handsome

The mums and dads who craft our 'matrimonial ads' carry on the tradition of seeking 'Fair, "bootyfull", "conventional", "earning" girl with homework skills for innocently-(preparing-for-IAS) divorced boy. Divorcees and widows, please excuse.'

But our new age lads are not like their dads. While they realize their booty may never be too full, or their homework too skilled, they are battling for gender-equality in at least one thing – fairness.

It's no secret that fairness is a national obsession, especially when looking for brides.

What has been kept a secret is that Indian men, too, rather like the idea of being fair. It took the launch of Emami's Fair and Handsome, in 2005, to pull that insight out from under the wraps. The first brand to see the potential in the men's fairness market, Emami. It saw an opportunity in the fact that quite a few fairness-cream users were male.[8] Clearly, men liked the thought of being fair, but they did not have any products to choose from.

---

[8] http://www.campaignindia.in/video/emami-relaunches-fair-and-handsome-with-srks-promise-of-more/419015

Every available product was targeted at women in their branding, messaging and packaging, effectively pushing male users into clandestine buying and usage. To its credit, Emami not only picked the right communication for its fairness product, it was subsequently responsible for launching a whole category of cosmetic products that helped give men a fair face.

The first stop was to support their claim that the product they had pioneered was, in reality, specifically formulated for male skin. And so came some fact-sharing. It appears that male skin is '20 per cent thicker' than women's skin and has more melanin. Male skin also abounds in that thing that women are constantly being judged on: pores. Turns out, men's pores are larger than women's pores![9]

But it doesn't end there for these pore guys. Larger pores also mean (as women have always suspected) that men are sweatier and oilier creatures.

All of this is unfortunate because a good complexion, they say, is key to making a good impression. Also, apparently, most women believe that men who groom their skin appear more confident.

But there was no cause for worry (and no need to steal your sister's or your mother's fairness cream anymore), because Emami's appropriately adjective-d Fair and Handsome cream with an advanced formulation, micro-absorbers and a great sun protection factor (SPF) would

---

[9] http://www.fairandhandsome.net/men-vs-women.html

result in effective sweat and oil control, dark spot reduction and, of course, fairness.

In 2005, Fair and Handsome had created a new category with its launch. Over the years, men began asking for more from their cream. In 2012, to bring about easy and wide acceptance, Emami decided to use an unquestionable role model. Someone who had earlier endorsed the product, someone masculine as well as handsome enough to make all the lovelies out there swoon over him – Shah Rukh Khan, the *baadshah* of Bollywood, a star at the top of his game whose appeal cut across genders and regions. Shah Rukh Khan epitomized the guy who wanted more out of life.

The ad starring Shah Rukh Khan opened with him talking about a time when he had first entered Bollywood, with no mentor to speak of and no one's legacy to lean on. All he could count on were his blessings. Watching stars go by strengthened his resolve to do well. So while others slept, he worked on polishing his acting skills. His dreams, and his wanting *zyaada* from life, were what drove him, and when he finally achieved what he wanted to it was with Fair and Handsome firmly by his side. Taking his legacy forward, he presents an awestruck fan with a tube of Fair and Handsome. The young man then shows the camera the actual results of using Fair and Handsome, and then the ad ends with Shah Rukh saying, 'World's Number One Emami Fair and Handsome. Because men want more.'

With changing times, the cream evolved as well, moving on to newer formulations. When the fairness range was taken forward to the Fair and Handsome face wash, none other than Hrithik Roshan, the alpha (to omega) male, was entrusted with the responsibility of endorsing it. As for winter skincare for men, Emami introduced a comprehensive Fair and Handsome Complete Winter Solution and a winter fairness cream in its fairness mix.

In 2013, the Indian men's fairness cream segment stood at around ₹329 crore. Now, competition to clean those clogged male pores includes brands like Garnier, Beiersdorf AG and Hindustan Unilever Ltd. It is estimated that the beauty, cosmetic and grooming market will be $20 billion by 2025[10], with a rapidly growing male skin-care segment. The fairness industry for men has seen intrepid fairness products march where no one had gone before. They have boldly rewritten the rules and helped closet fair-and-handsomes come galloping out in droves.

If life was a fairy tale, these guys could Also, apparently, most that magic mirror on the wall, who was the fairest of them all? Maybe the mirror would tell them 'Oye, it's you, *chikney*.'

Radio Mirchi

Many decades ago, All India Radio (AIR) gifted Indians a line with which to instantly shame a crying child into silence: '*Chup! Shuroo ho gayi* All India Radio.'

[10] 'Personal Care Market to Touch $20 Billion in India by 2025', *Business Standard*, 8 July 2016

For some time there, AIR was the only representative of radio as a medium in India. It was the country's source of all things interesting, be it music, news or general entertainment.

Of course, we didn't want our actual All India Radio to shut up at all. It was omnipresent and it was AIR that probably spawned our habit of constantly playing film songs in the background – with the volume at low when our kids were asleep, and with the volume on high when it was only the neighbours who were asleep.

Radio caught India's ear in 1923. While the British were trying not to Quit India, the Radio Club of Bombay had its own agenda. It began broadcasting programmes, earning its place as a marker in our history. All India Radio (AIR) came into being in 1936, replacing what used to be called the Indian State Broadcasting Service (ISBS), a service controlled by the colonial government. When India became independent, Delhi, Bombay, Calcutta, Madras, Lucknow and Tiruchirappalli accounted for the country's six radio stations.

Radio broadcasting used to be such a miraculous thing that it seemed absolutely apt to think of it as a celestial gift, nothing less than the voice from the sky. Yes, *yeh akashvani hai*. It was radio that gave ear-glue to the nation, it lent the neighbourhood *paanwalla* (always from Benaras) his trademark prop, and of course it was what many *antakshari* experts owed their skills to.

Till 1993, radio had always meant only one thing to Indians – AIR. A government undertaking, it was the only broadcaster in India. Then the government decided to privatize the radio broadcasting sector and sold airtime blocks on its FM channels. (FM was the modern-sounding abbreviation for the decidedly un-sexy technical term – frequency modulation.)

FM radio, which commanded an ever-growing following, saw Delhi NCR and Maharashtra emerging as leading markets. This continued growth has been instrumental in making most marketers increase the amount they spend on radio advertising. To companies operating in India's FM radio market, all this bodes well. Prasar Bharati, Entertainment Network India Limited, Sun TV Network Limited, Reliance Broadcast Network Limited, Music Broadcast Private Limited and D.B. Corp Limited are among those that rule the roost. And, through the years, channels like Big FM, Red FM, Radio One, Fever FM, Oye FM and Vividh Bharati have all vied for attention.

And then there is Radio Mirchi from the Times Group, which is one brand that has often managed to surprise with its advertising. The Times Group first began with Times FM in 1993 and provided for many listeners their first brush with FM radio itself. It was owned by the Entertainment Network India Ltd (ENIL), one of the subsidiaries of the Times Group. This was the time when radio in India began to reinvent itself with engaging content in terms of music as well as presentation.

When in 2000, the government auctioned 108 FM frequencies across India, ENIL bagged the largest number of frequencies. As the poster-child for radio 'hotness', the channel was named Radio Mirchi. 'It's hot,' you were told. As the government gave out more licences over the years, the portfolio grew. In the beginning of 2017, ENIL was looking at 74 frequencies in 64 cities.[11]

While the brand's overall objective was to increase reach, there was also the need to keep its constantly evolving audience engaged. Since then, innovative content and branding become key to Radio Mirchi's marketing. It continuously conceptualized new shows and capsules, and created a persona that listeners seemed to like.

Tapping into the core connect that music has, Radio Mirchi projects itself as the brand that makes people feel happy. That is, a Radio Mirchi listener is upbeat and has *joie de vivre*: '*Mirchi sunnewale* always *khush*.'

Early on, Mirchi chose to take the route of showcasing optimism and joy in an obviously messy situation – so much so that one of the first few commercials in 2005 tailored around this thought had a sewer worker break out into a happy song because he was listening to Radio Mirchi.

By 2015, the radio industry in India was at ₹2,300 crore and was looking to be more than double in the coming years. While this was a small number when compared

---

[11] 'Radio Mirchi Buys 21 New Frequencies in FM Auctions', 28 February 2017

to print and television, it boded well for players like Radio Mirchi.

Radio Mirchi was already a very visible brand with tons of properties like the Mirchi Top 20 playlists, the Spell Bee competition held across many cities, and the Mirchi Music Awards' ceremonies for excellence in Hindi music. Interesting content, the stickiness of the brand and RJs with individual fandoms kept people tuning in.

But by this time, there was a new challenge facing it – the growing fondness for streaming music, especially among the youth. It became necessary for Radio Mirchi to build brand recall. With its plans of entering new markets within the country, the channel was very aware of the need to attract youngsters back to radio, and more specifically to itself. So it came up with a brand new commercial. Even after almost ten years, '*Mirchi sunnewale* always *khush*,' as a thought, had resonance. So once again the communication focused on it and showed a study in contrasts.

The main characters in their commercial were *rudaalis*, those paid-for mourners traditionally from Rajasthan. Summoned to cry at a funeral, the older *rudaali* finds that her team of young wailers just can't seem to deliver on the weeping front. When they do cry, it just doesn't hit the spot. The gathered family and villagers are understandably miffed and the old *rudaali*'s reputation is getting seriously damaged. Even as more tragedies and punishments unfold, the young women remain incomprehensibly dry-eyed. In the end, they take pity on the older woman and reveal to her that they have had their earphones plugged in and have been listening to Radio Mirchi all this time. And, of course, *Mirchi sunne waale* always *khush*. (Goes to show that happy employees are not always good for business.) The film ends on the older woman dancing – to music playing on Radio Mirchi.

The communication introduced laughter into a dodgy situation, created for itself colossal recall value, and bridged the generational and the urban-rural divide all in one go, and with tongue tucked firmly in cheek.

This was all part of the Radio Mirchi vibe, contributing to the 'It's hot' appeal. Today, Radio Mirchi figures among the top three radio channels across India. It is No. 1 in many cities and has an enviable listenership.

Yes, radio. Someone still loves you.

Kurkure

Whoever said that the East is East and the West is West and never shall the twain meet, had obviously never met a bag of Kurkure.

Kurkure's PepsiCo parentage was unmistakably pardesi, but its nationality was definitely desi. It was, quite literally, a twisted piece of work – one that made the snacking community in India do a double-take.

Made from rice, corn and lentils, the sqiggly Kurkure was launched by PepsiCo as a new snack in 1999. Specifically made for India, it pitted itself as a packaged option to both the premium chips' brands and the economical, branded *namkeen* brigade. Kurkure had two tantalizing charms – a larger pack-size and a lower price. And, of course, it tasted great too. In fact, a key effort was made in coming up with innovative flavours and, over the years, flavours like Masala Munch, Naughty Tomato, Green Chutney Rajasthani Style, Hyderabadi Hungama, Chilli Chatka were introduced.

Right from the beginning, the name itself suggested a crunchy snacking experience. Going by how quickly Kurkure became popular, and how yummy people found it, the advertising line '*Kya karein*, control *nahin hota!*' seemed apt. For some time, it seemed an efficient enough expression for the brand. Since likeability didn't seem to be a problem, it was time to up consumption by associating it with occasions when people got together – like family chai times.

In 2001, Kurkure aired a commercial that was all about a control-freak of a matriarch declaring to a new *bahu* (who is seen dishing up a new pack of Kurkure) that the household was all about restraint. Even as she issues diktats about eating, behaving and generally being in control, she notices that her family members are not just snacking on Kurkure more than they should but (as a result) also giggling and definitely being much more joyful than they should. Her husband addresses her bewilderment at not being in control by offering her some Kurkure along with the advice to abandon this control-*shantrol* and become '*kha ke mast*'.

Basically '*Masti* equals Kurkure' was the space the brand appropriated for the next few years. In 2005, it brought on board actress Juhi Chawla as its effervescent brand ambassador. Getting her to spoof the character, Tulsi, from the popular TV soap, *Kyunki Saas Bhi Kabhi Bahu Thi*, the brand told people, '*Kahani mein kuchh kurkura hona chahiye.*'

But, come 2007, a mad genius of an enemy began rearing its oddly-shaped head – Bingo! from ITC Foods. It had a quirky worldview, tasted great and had intriguing (product) shapes like *Tedhe Medhe* and Mad Angles. Something needed to be done to counter it.

Thus came about an endearing, engaging and (some say) double-meaning expression. '*Tedha hai par mera hai*,' claimed the Kurkure ad the following year, focusing a bit on its own shape. Kurkure decided to capture the very essence of the product as well as the consumer by showing quintessentially Indian situations and people's acceptance of the way things are – imperfections and oddities included.

In 2008, its television commercial showed an arranged marriage meet-up where the actress Juhi Chawla plays a spunky Punjabi housewife trying to get her relative, Montu, married. But as the bespectacled, buck-toothed, degree-less Montu appears decidedly *tedha*, the father of the bride remains adamant that he is not quite the son-in-law they had in mind. Then the band plays a rousing tune and Montu throws his shirt into the ring (literally) and dances with abandon, his abs rippling and body moving in perfect coordination.

This twist in the tale leads to Montu receiving a two-thumbs-up from the girl (much to the consternation of her moustachioed father), indicating that she wholly accepted his *tedha*-ness.

One film focused on *tedha* families. There is the grandson who grandfather admits is '*khota*' (that is, defective) but, whattodo, he is after all the '*pota*'; a woman who knows her husband is slow but he is still her '*woh*'. There is even a ghost who poses in the family photo because though she is *swargwaasi,* she is the *maasi*.

The fun ads continued over the years. As Indians munched their way through fast-selling packs of Kurkure, you could hear them agree that '*tedha hai par mera hai*'. The phrase crept into popular lingo and could well have been the caption to Kurkure's not-quite-*seedha* career-path itself. It had pioneered its way into the *namkeen*/chips market, it had forced folks to sit up and take notice and it had gotten itself included as a legitimate partner of the Diwali *mithai* (smartly increasing its consumption base too).

Knowing that innovations were key, it not only came up with competitive variants like Kurkure Triangles, its twisted brandings kept getting more and more *purab-paschim* – from flavours like *Rajma* and *Achaar* to Andhra Bangkok Curry, Rajasthani Manchurian and even Punjabi Pizza. The success of Kurkure also inspired a whole host of local crunchy-munchies – Crax from DFM Foods, the Gujarat-based Balaji and Indore's Yellow Diamond among them.

Bridging the space between traditional and Westernized salted snacks, Kurkure dominated its category in India. Not content with its success, however, it set off to conquer other shores.

So now, not only is it making our Bangladeshi and Pakistani *bhais*' mouths *kurkura*, it is doing the same in markets such as Canada, UAE and the Gulf too. (As Indians, we have taken great personal pride in this bit of corporate affair-ing by a made-in-India product. After all, the prodigious child seems so much more talented when he 'goes *abraad*'.)

Who knows, this may just turn out to be a *tedha* tale of how the West was won.

Maggi Hot & Sweet

In the mid-1980s, when Maggi entered the tomato ketchup category, the existing players in the market like Kissan and Volfarm were all touting the freshness of their *laal*, *raseelay* and *gol-gol tamatar*. The consumer was hooked to his tomato sauce brands but flirting with chilli sauce on the side. So while the market share of tomato sauce was healthy, there was opportunity in spicing things up. Enter Maggi Hot & Sweet Tomato Chilli Sauce. Tangy and sweet, with a sharp hint of chilli, it had all the tomatoey goodness that the Westernized product demanded but with the added oomph that made it pretty much an Indian crowd-pleaser.

Just as crowd-pleasing were the ads starring veteran actor Pankaj Kapoor and comedian Javed Jaffrey. They showed the duo in caricatured interactions which revolved around Maggi Hot & Sweet Tomato Chilli Sauce. The ads always ended with a hyper Jaffrey demanding to know, '*Aakhir iss* sauce *mein different kya hai*?'

In some ad films, Jaffrey was styled like yesteryear Bollywood villain, Ajit – a don complete with Western clothes, trademark drawl and a ditzy moll. In newly independent India, Ajit had been a popular *filmi* villain – the wolf in Western clothing. In the Maggi ads, he again provided the perfect foil for the *teekha*-loving traditionalist.

One of the best-remembered ads was shot around the theme 'One day with Lily'. Jaffrey was seen getting his nails filed by said Lily while outlining how their *helikaapter* would soon land far from the Hindustan *baarder*. Just as he is seen telling Michael (his minion, played by Kapoor) to get on his cycle, Kapoor thumps a bottle down on a table. Startled, the don leaps up and asks, '*Saara shahar mujhe* Lion [pronounced 'loin'] *ke naam se jaanta hai aur tum ye kambakht tamaatar ka sauce khaate rehte ho?*' Kapoor tells him that, boss, it was not just tomato sauce, it was 'Maggi Hot & Sweet Tomato Chilli Sauce. It's different.' On being questioned exasperatedly about said difference, Kapoor shrugs and says, 'This *soss* is different, Boss.' The girl giggles and the don tells her, 'Lily, don't be silly.' 'Enjoy the difference', you were told in the end.

Another film was titled, 'One day at night'. Jaffrey, as mafioso, dreams of Kapoor mopping up sauce with bread. This is a nightmare apparently, because he wakes up with a start, babbling about sauce. On hearing this, Kapoor happily takes out his personal bottle while correcting the boss by saying that it wasn't a sauce, it was 'Maggi Hot & Sweet Tomato Chilli Sauce. It's different.' At this point, the frustrated Jaffrey leaps right through a wall – or, as the moll says, 'Boss has gone for a toss.'

Then there was 'One day at a tennis match'. In choreographed motion, the audience's eyes are seen following the rhythmic to-and-fro of the tennis ball, even as a similarly mesmerized Jaffrey comments on tennis being *the* game, what with the weather, the crowd... This is when out comes Kapoor's sauce bottle from which he pours sauce liberally over his two samosas. Distracted from the game, Jaffrey irritably asks what was so special about the tomato sauce that it had even accompanied them to a match. To which Kapoor corrects him, saying that it wasn't a tomato sauce, it was 'Maggi Hot & Sweet Tomato Chilli Sauce. It's different.' Exasperated, Javed screams out loud, asking if anyone could tell him what the difference really was, only to have the entire audience screaming, 'It's different!' back at him.

The film that opened on a vacuous-looking Jaffrey in a hospital because he had lost his *mammory* (as Kapoor put it) was also much-loved. Kapoor tries reminding him of familiar things – the park, bench, film, tennis match, *sau din* sauce *ke* – but nothing seems to be working...until he waves a bottle in front of Jaffrey. Immediately, Jaffrey's eyes fix themselves on the bottle even as he starts mumbling what sounds like 'sauce'. This is when Kapoor interrupts him, saying it wasn't a sauce, it was 'Maggi Hot & Sweet Tomato Chilli Sauce. It's different.' On hearing this, Jaffrey's brain seems to short-circuit while he springs into action, cart-wheeling right off screen. Chuckling knowingly, Kapoor holds the bottle up saying, 'Maggi Hot & Sweet Tomato Chilli Sauce. It's different.'

The films always ended with the voiceover telling you to enjoy the difference. Chock-full of PJs and puns, the fun ads quickly became a rage. Today, they are as much a part of folklore as the Ajith jokes some of them took inspiration from.

While Javed Jaffrey and Pankaj Kapoor became instantly identifiable with the product, the ads played a big role in helping the brand achieve an iconic status. The punny jokes spawned many fans. The scripts, reportedly written by Javed Jaffrey himself, entered drawing-room and water-cooler conversations.

That Indians, with their reputation for liking fiery, spicy food, would like Maggi Hot & Sweet Tomato Chilli Sauce was a no-brainer. But while the name of the sauce itself held promise, it was the communication that imprinted itself on people's minds with the 'It's different' campaign.

Soon, the sauce was a market leader. Or, as Jaffrey said in one of the commercials, *saara shahar* knew it as the 'lion'.

To conclude, it must be said that while many modern brands cater to our Indian-ness – some with their product-features, and some with their communication – sometimes the Indian-ness is just a visual prop.

A few decades ago, for those who in the twilight zone between cycle and scooter, there was the ubiquitous, economical, just-right-for-India '*Chal meri* Luna' moped.

Fevicol showed you the everyday Indian spectacle of an eye-popping number of people literally piled on to a vehicle, even as it made its hi-tech promise, '*Yeh* Fevicol *ka majboot jod hai, tootega nahin.*'

Happydent White chewing gum made a human chandelier out of a guy. His teeth were so white (because of his cutting-edge chewing gum) that he was capable of lighting up an extremely ornate Indian setting merely by smiling.

Putting a modern twist on a familiar scenario is a favourite as Brandjis Turn Mod.

But whether they are BTM or MTB, in India products and ads can take on very interesting *avatars*.

Because we are pretty interesting as a people.

Where else in the world will you find a *Banno* whose 'swagger *laage seksy!*'?

Or a James Bond who isn't allowed to kiss?

Digital, Widgetal and App toh Aise Na The

COOL TOOLS

For centuries, we have been searching for the meaning of life. Today, we are still searching – but this time it's for Sunny Leone.

A few years ago, the (former) adult film star was the most Googled person in our country, followed by the actor Salman Khan and the erstwhile president of India, A.P.J. Abdul Kalam.

But let it not be said that we do not have our priorities straight...because several million of us are also piously looking for holy matrimony online (the practical ones are scouring matrimonial sites slyly looking for dates).

Meanwhile, many of us who are sick of spending our lives looking for love, (or career prospects or shopping *dhamakas*), are awakening our inner Jedi and using augmented reality to play with lightsabers, *Star Wars* style.

Gaming, watching videos, downloading, sharing, surfing, shopping, tweeting, Instagramming, romancing – the Indian online is pretty active and engaged.

In fact, India is quite a leader when it comes to the number of people who access the Internet on their phones. As of 31 December 2016, India had 391.5 million Internet subscribers according to the Telecom Regulatory Authority of India (TRAI). By 2020, an estimated 730 million Indians will be on the Internet.[1]

So while not sizeable in proportion to the population (what *is* really?), the number of Indians online forms a

---

[1] Goliya, Kshitiz, 'India to Have 730 Million Internet Users By 2020, Says Report', *Livemint*, 17 August 2016

pretty significant audience. When it comes to mobile penetration, Internet and technology adoption, the country is considered to be one of the fastest growing economies in the world.

No wonder, then, that as India stands with a come-hither look in the eyes and a device in the hand, the collective heads of marketing moguls globally turn to look.

It also makes for some very interesting case studies.

KFC

Reality sucks, right? Which is why your friendly neighbourhood marketer has been getting you augmented reality.

Augmented reality (AR), while not new, has enormous potential for marketers. Brands are still experimenting with the technology, and coming up with ideas to suit their markets. With the real world colliding unexpectedly with the digital world, the possibilities are endless after all. But while it may be interesting for the consumer to point his smartphone camera at an ad/poster/character/whatever and watch it come to life, one important detail lies in getting them to point that camera in the first place.

Undaunted by the challenge, though, KFC embraced AR and used it pretty effectively to enhance customer experience in its restaurants.

Based in Louisville, Kentucky, KFC Corporation is one of the world's most popular chicken restaurant chains, with multiple outlets in more than a hundred countries. But be that as it may, the discerning Indian needed convincing when KFC came to the country in 1995. After all, while all of us appreciate a good Chicken 65 from South India, nothing gets North India more worked up than its *tandoori* chicken. Some would argue that said chicken should be the national bird of Punjab. So yeah, the world may have been eating this KFC chicken but we liked our local leg-*wegg* with our *daaru ka* peg.

But that was then.

Today, even in India, if you say 'fried chicken', chances are that KFC will come to mind. KFC's batter-fried, crispy favourites and India-inspired innovations (like rice bowlz) have been catering to customers through hundreds of their outlets across the country. And yes, there has even been a fiery grilled or *tandoori* chicken equivalent, thank you very much. Let it not be said that they didn't aim to please.

So why the innovations? Who were they even competing against?

India had long been in the sights of fast-food/quick-service restaurant chains and this had resulted in many major chains rushing to set up shop in the country. All this meant is that there were now more suitors for every customer who had to be wooed. It became a constant battle for the fair consumer's hand (or mouth).

Being two of biggest fast-food chains in the world, KFC and McDonald's had faced off innumerable times at innumerable places. This trend continued in India, where

McDonald's arch and KFC's Colonel Sanders logo became familiar, recognizable sights and were sometimes found metres away from each other, trying to entice customers.

Then there were the familiar menu items of one posing as new dishes in the other. KFC, known for its chicken, had its zinger burger vying for a place in the burger popularity charts, whereas McDonald's – traditionally known for its burgers – had its own version of chicken strips.

Often, the fight boiled down to price. It is safe to say that (perceived) value-for-money offerings were known to tempt the customer, who was an extremely fickle creature. To keep this creature happy, in 2013, McDonald's introduced its 'Happy Price' menu, offering dishes for just ₹25. Not to be outdone, KFC launched a ₹25 deal as well – one that targeted young people and college kids for whom being economical was a big consideration. This, despite the fact that, until then, KFC's target audience was adults in their late twenties – a consumer base with serious potential because a large chunk of India's population is under thirty years old.

KFC decided to highlight the ₹25 deal and use it as an opportunity to expand its consumer base. It aired a television commercial for a new 'Wow Menu', in which prices ranged from ₹25 to ₹69.

The ad film opened on three youngsters standing outside a KFC outlet, drooling over the food inside. As young people often are, they were broke and therefore hadn't been to KFC for days. And that was when the 'Wow Menu' dramatically entered their lives with its life-altering food range that started at just ₹25, enabling them to eat happily (ever after). '25 *mein khao, khake bolo* WOW', KFC told people.

So far, so traditional.

Then came the real star of the marketing campaign – the all-new augmented reality app on offer called WOW@25.

KFC decided to build its campaign around the fact that their consumer base was young and always on their smartphones. What if this could be used to facilitate interaction with the brand?

With the WOW@25 app, the consumer could scan a currency note – any note from ₹10 to ₹1,000 would do – and a 3D animation would come to life. The app would suggest various meal combos or standalone items that could be ordered for the denomination of the note that had been scanned.

Once the app was launched, it was made available on both Android and iOS platforms. The app also had a fun quiz that helped the consumer construct their order without getting confused by the in-store options.

KFC also leveraged its social media and digital presence to really spread the word. The 2.7 million people following KFC on Facebook and the 3,000 on Twitter were invited to solve the KFC Wow Quiz on their phones or on the Internet. The marketing effort also included outdoor, radio and in-store collaterals.

Within twenty days, the KFC WOW@25 app was downloaded over 35,000 times on mobile phones while the microsite got over 150,000 visits.[2] To add to the triumph, at the 18th Webby People's Voice Awards held in 2014 in New York, 'Wow @ 25' was the only Indian winner.

To think that, just a few decades ago, television was all we had to augment our reality with. And now, who knows, on a day like say Karva Chauth, a woman may soon augment reality by ditching the *chhani* and looking hungrily at the moon ('Look, look, it's delicious and was actually made of cheese all along!') through her smartphone camera, of course. And then look at her spouse ('Look look, he too is delicious and was actually Shah Rukh Khan all along'), again through her smartphone camera, of course.

Tinder

Not only do Indians have 'family values' type of notions about themselves, it appears that match-making companies have the same notions about their users. They seem to believe that:

- Indians don't have premarital sex. (Or extramarital sex for that matter.)
- Indians definitely do not look for no-strings-attached sex.
- Indian mummy-papas give full-full blessings before the kids set out on dating endeavours.

---

[2] Bhattacharyaa, Anushree, 'Hunger Games', *Financial Express*, 10 December 2013

The last viewpoint may possibly apply to matrimonial sites – where there is tacit acceptance that some dating may be allowed under the watchful eyes of the mummy-daddies who have invariably created their darling *baccha*'s profile. However, the fact of the matter is that many young Indians have moved on. (In fact, some of the stalwarts of the matrimonial services in India have moved on too. To the divorced person wondering about his/her chances on shaadi.com, there is secondshaadi.com)

While some of India is scouring matrimonial sites hoping to accidentally bump into someone special, people are also purposely bumping into each other on sites designed specifically for that, umm, bumping purpose.

And while some countries have reached a saturation point when it comes to online dating, India, with its teeming billions, is seen as the next big Lovers Lane (as of 2016, 6 million singles had joined dating sites).[3]

Dating sites are not always the playgrounds of only speed daters, one-night-standers and looking-for-love(rs). Since *pyaar* knows no boundaries and Cupid's arrows look a lot like the computer cursor, honest-to-God romance can be found in the virtual world too.

While authenticity and safety are a concern, dating apps do provide a meeting ground where people can scout

---

[3] Bhandaram, Vishnupriya, 'Truly, Madly, Deeply Rai Bareilli', *Firstpost*, 14 February 2016

for what interests them – like-mindedness, common pursuits and short-term or long-term partners.

As of now, there are a growing number of apps that offer dating services (and they can get incredibly specific in their offerings). You can Thrill, you can Woo, you can even Vee. Don't forget to iCrushiFlush, go QuackQuack, get Hinge(d), TrulyMadly, EkCoffee, Matchify, OKCupid, Bloomy, HookedUp, Kama, Bumble, Moco or Aisle. There are also real-time curated events organized by companies like Floh, Mix & Mingle, Footloose No More and Sirf Coffee. Why, even Shaadi.com has entered the online dating market with Frivil.

The Tinder app was launched in 2012. By 2015, it was present in almost 196 countries in around 30 languages. Among the first few swiping apps available to iOS and Android users, it soon became *the* location-based dating app.

Meanwhile, burger chains to beer brands, shoemakers to fashion labels had all been narrowing down on the country as the next big market. Tinder was no exception. Seeing great potential in the thousands of people who were acquiring smartphones every day in India, Tinder arrived for our singles (and some of our doubles) in 2013.

By 2015, the app saw a stunning 400 per cent increase in downloads compared to the year before. Approximately 90 per cent of Tinder users in India were between 18 and 34 in age; interestingly, of these, women seemed to be more active than men (in sending 'super likes').[4]

One of the primary reasons for the app's popularity was possibly its easy-to-use interface. Once installed, the app picked up your Facebook information as your profile. (Which often gave rise to some astonishing scenarios like wondering who in the group profile picture from Facebook was the Tinder user, or even seeing a user posing unwittingly with their boyfriend/girlfriend/spouse.) It then scanned the area around a user and picked out other users according to the primary user's preferences.

The user swiped left to move from one photo to the next, and swiped right on seeing someone likeable. If two users liked each other, they got 'matched' and could then chat. In just a few years, with billions of matches behind it, Tinder had gained a reputation. And though longer relationships were not unknown, the perception of Tinder was that of a hook-up app.

In 2016, Tinder talked of India being its topmost market in Asia and among the largest five markets in its global network.[5] Since it now had a strong presence in metro cities, the company decided to expand its base in the country. While globally Tinder mostly relied on

---

[4] 'Tinder's Downloads in India Up 400%; Women More Active', *The Hindu*, 25 November 2015

[5] Chaturvedi, Anumeha, 'India Is the Largest Market for Tinder in Asia: Taru Kapoor, Head, India, Tinder', *Economic Times*, 15 April 2016

word-of-mouth to promote its app, it decided to venture into uncharted territory in India.

Moving away from its image of matching people for casual hook-ups, Tinder decided to do a U-turn and appeal to Indians using what they thought we loved best – *sanskaar*.

Tinder aired a television commercial which showed a young woman getting ready to go out. Just then, her mother enters the room. As Mom sits on the bed looking at her daughter, the girl's phone buzzes. On looking at it, Mom sees a Tinder notification flashing on the screen. *Hawwwww*?

Naaaah! Without blinking an eyelash, she tells her daughter that she approves – that is, 'swipes right' on the guy. The ad film ends with the message: 'It's how people meet.'

On its Facebook page, Tinder posted the ad film saying, 'The people we meet and the connections we forge change our lives. Tinder is how everyone today meets new, like-minded people around them – people who become friends, lovers, mentors, acquaintances, partners, movie-buddies or soulmates. #SwipeRight to a world of possibilities.'

Right.

If the intent for Tinder was to be part of the conversation around dating, it certainly succeeded. The ad film was shared extensively on Twitter and Facebook.

But the overwhelming reaction to the ad was surprise. People felt that Tinder was trying to reinvent its core and legitimize its usage by creating an Indianized version for its audience. More than a few sniggers did the rounds too. Some wondered whether it would actually make the audience turn away from the brand.

The overall feeling was that Tinder may just have made the 'mother' of all dating ads. But making Tinder a sort of mummy-approved dating service was just not going to cut it.

Isee liye Mummy *ne meri tujhe* Tinder *pe bulaaya hai?*

Uff, swipe left.

Amazon

Online shopping sites are wonderful places. Where else would you think of, let alone find, a Made-For-Her ball pen (after all, pens had been so harsh on women before), a banana slicer (a revolution in fruity experiences), a mini-mango tree, imported (no less), and pure cow-dung cakes.

It's the shop that never closes with the sale that never ends and the products that never fail to grip. It's exactly what the 'great Indian shopper' ordered. And no one knows this better than the e-commerce sites that have set up shop in the country.

India was often being touted as the world's fastest growing e-commerce market – what with investments increasing and Internet users growing. To add to the excitement, smartphones were increasingly being bought and used, bringing more and more consumers into the marketplace.

It was only a matter of time before Amazon, the world's most formidable Internet-based retailer, took notice.

Amazon was launched in 1994 as an online bookstore in Seattle. In a few years, it became the largest e-commerce player in the USA with separate websites for the UK and for Canada, among other countries. Racing ahead of the times with talk of delivery drones and self-check-out stores, it also built a folklore-ish narrative around the genius of its founder and how it was changing the world as we knew it.

Amazon had stated that its vision was to be Earth's most customer-centric company; to build a place where people could come to find and discover virtually anything they wanted to buy online. Their endeavour was to give customers more of what they wanted – a vast selection, low prices, fast and reliable delivery, and a trusted and convenient online shopping experience. It also provided sellers a world-class e-commerce platform to reach their buyers and had millions of products under many categories including clothing, jewellery, beauty products, furniture, ebooks and paper books.

In 2013, having arrived in India, Amazon needed to gain insight into the Indian consumer's online habits and needs. Their competitors were already in place in the form of Flipkart, eBay, Jabong, SnapDeal, Myntra and others, each one of them already on Hello, Hi-Buy terms with Indians.

Amazon decided to target both existing and new users – 18- to 45-year-olds who had access to the Internet, liked a good buy and loved variety. They concentrated on creating a great shopping experience with better functionality, attractive delivery promises and endless choice.

The need to see more options and to choose only after getting the best value for their money plays a vital role in Indian buying decisions. As kids, we have all hung our mortified heads when Radha Aunty and Mummy have sailed out of sari stores ('No variety!') after getting the entire stock out of the shelves and draped on an assortment of sales boys. And then we have grown up to do exactly the same. Why buy a tomato without first checking every tomato seller's wares in the *mandi*? Same pinch for television sets. Or cars.

This need for 'variety' has traditionally been a cornerstone of the Indian consumer's buying behaviour. The expression of this need is in a few immortal phrases: '*Aur hai kya?*', '*Kuchh aur?*' or '*Aur dikhao*'.

This was the insight that Amazon played up in their messaging. They decided to make their campaign about customers getting unlimited options for their budget, however limited that budget might be.

The television commercial presented a mixed bag of situations, some funny, all relatable. A man, just home from work, happily goes for some cake in the refrigerator, when he is reminded by his stern-faced wife that it is *karva chauth* (that is, she was fasting for *his* long life). This makes the guilty husband log on to Amazon to find gifts, gifts and more gifts. A family on vacation is shown picture-after-picture-after-picture of all the places they could visit but want more options. The matriarch of a family aboard a flight hands out snacks – *dhokla*, *thepla*, *khakhra*, *fafda*, *muthiya*, *mathiya*...and so on – even as someone asks to see more. A Sikh boy copies the dancing styles of many different actors in Bollywood films – because his audience wants to see more (...Sallu, Hrithik, Shahid, Aamir, Shah Rukh, *jitne super star hain sabki, Nakal hume karke dikhlaao, Hindustani darshak bole, oye puttar, aur dikhao...*). A man holds a distressed baby while his wife comforts the child by showing him different products on Amazon because, '*Janam siddh adhikar hai chunna, kum me* settle *na hona, munna.*' And so it went on.

A montage of such situations was held together by a jingle which played up Indian idiosyncrasies quite amusingly, the main message being the refrain, '*Hindustani dil kehta hai, aur dikhao, aur dikhao.*'

This was followed by Amazon asking people to download their app and enjoy the abundance of choices. That the brand was successful in engaging people was clear from the number of jokes the ad films spawned. (One likened it to Delhi University where even if one admission-aspirant had got 98 per cent and another had 98.8 per cent, the University would keep asking '*aur dikhao*'.) Even as the campaign rolled out, Amazon steadily increased the number of vendors on the site so the '*aur dikhao*' promise held true. Sales increased. And Amazon, a relative newcomer, became one of the most visited e-commerce sites in India.

Television ads took centre stage with print and outdoors being used to augment the messaging. The spot played over and over during the IPL season. Amazon also focused on its digital and social presence. Their Twitter handle was changed to #AurDikhao, and they used it to talk to brands and celebrities. They also tweeted about the campaign, used the account to make contest announcements and to make people interact and laugh with them.

Notably, the brand engaged with Twitter influencers. It asked Baba Sehgal to *dikhao* more of his funny jokes. And it asked Kanan Gill to review more new movies on his popular YouTube channel.

All in all, the messaging was funny, the situations were relatable and the jingle was extremely hummable. Running contests and tweeting to celebrities and brands kept Amazon's messaging fresh in their consumers' minds. Moreover, while pulling the collective Indian leg about their shopping behaviour, it did not make fun of Indians. It made us laugh at ourselves while making the point about shopping smart with Amazon very clear.

Amazon, *aur* ads *dikhao*, could well have been the sentiment after this particular piece of communication.

Groupon

(Or how it became Groupon.ion.)

When Groupon.com, the big daddy of deal-a-day websites entered the Indian market in 2011, people were already questioning the business model itself. What's more, there were already many hopefuls in the e-commerce market – SnapDeal, Taggle, Buzzintown, MyDala, Dealivore, DealsAndYou.com, Koovs and MobStreet, to name a few.

All these sites featured a multitude of must-have stuff and discounted gift certificates valid at local or national outlets of spas, restaurants, diagnostic labs, events, among others. Understandably, competition was stiff.

But at the right time and place, some product deals have what it takes to be a blockbuster. In September 2013, the onion was just such a product.

At that time, onions were selling for as much as eighty to a hundred rupees a kilo. In a country where people have been known to ask for onions on the side with their pizza, this portends terrible times. '*Sarkar giregi*', was the doleful consensus of a population rumoured to be in the practice of kicking out governments on the basis of onion prices (remember the 1998 Delhi elections?).

Groupon decided to show its pizzazz with the pyaaz. It began selling onions at ₹9 a kilo for a whole week, for a maximum of 3,000 kilos of onions to be sold everyday. It proved to be a move that brought about onion-induced tears of joy, and consumers lapped up the deal. Those who did not see the offer on Groupon pounced on it when they came across it on social media platforms.

Google searches for Groupon increased by 400 per cent the day the deal was launched. Within six days, there were 22,727 transactions on their website which translated into over 15,000 new customer registrations.[6]

On the first day, the onion deal had been unveiled through a series of teasers on the Groupon India Facebook page. They also held a contest on Twitter. A Google Nexus tab was offered to funny tweets with the hashtag #Onionify. This managed to get into the top 10 India Twitter trends. In three days, #Onionify generated more than 3,000 conversations and created an exposure of 2.79 million. So much so, that major publications like the *Wall Street Journal*, *Business Standard* and the *Economic Times* also covered the offer.

All of this gave Groupon a bigger reach, amplified its traffic and gave it a strong-on-deals branding. Within forty minutes of the announcement, the stock was sold. The second day, online traffic was such that it caused the website to crash. On the seventh day, within ten minutes of going live, the deal had sold out for the day.

Though a one-off episode in the brand story, what a tear-jerker it turned out to be. A pungent episode in marketing if ever there was one.

Garnier Men's

Some things are an Indian phenomenon. Like our chicken tikka masala, our Rajnikanth jokes and

[6] Bhagat, Rasheeda, 'How Groupon Sold Onions at Rs. 9 a Kg', *The Hindu Business Line*, 21 September 2013

our love for missed calls. Relationships have been based on, '*Jaanoo*, give me a missed call when college is over.' Mothers-in-law have been known to ask errant *bahus*, 'I gave you a missed call. Why didn't you give a call-back?' Impoverished students have told their parents, 'I'll give you a missed call when you need to send me money.'

And brands have used it in India to entice customers with, 'Give me a missed call and I'll show you the world.' Or I'll show you an IPL player. Or an ad. They call it 'Missed Call Marketing' – a special way of operating in a unique country. (Though, as a marketing tool, missed calls are also used in Latin America as well as in Africa, where it is called flashing or beeping.)

In India, many brands have used it, including Active Wheel, Saffola Life, Set Wet and Colgate, to name a few. That the method has long-term possibilities has been made obvious by missed call marketing platforms like ZipDial and VivaConnect being acquired and partnered by Twitter and Facebook respectively.

When they respond to an ad, customers call the number given but hang up before connecting. It is the company that then calls back with deals, promotional offers or even entertainment capsules interspersed with product messages.

The advertiser does pay for the cost of returning the call to the telecom operator but the return on this investment is worth it. Companies get to collect data on a customer's interests, which makes for customized advertising. Bonding is quick and live and a reciprocating community can be built for desired periods of time.

Garnier Men is just such an example of missed call marketing.

In the fast-growing men's grooming category, Garnier Men, the personal care and grooming brand from the cosmetics company, L'Oreal, was one of the key contenders. In 2014, it was also the official partner for Rajasthan Royals and Sunrisers Hyderabad, which were both franchises in the wildly popular Indian Premier League.

In partnership with ZipDial, Facebook created an ad for Garnier Men which ran from April to May. The target audience would see the ad on their Facebook newsfeed, asking them to give a missed call to a toll-free number. Just clicking on the ad would trigger the call, which automatically disconnected after a couple of rings. Consumers would then receive an SMS with a link to participate in a contest which gave them the opportunity to win merchandise or even meet the Rajasthan Royals. There was also another link that helped them purchase the products online.

Basically, Garnier Men went one-to-one with its consumers, wanting to reinforce its brand association with the IPL and exploit the hype around it. The aim was not only to get more participation in the brand's IPL contest, it was to get people to log in to Flipkart which is where they were e-tailing and, of course, to increase sales.

To that effect, Facebook said that 15 million people were reached with the missed-call-ins and online sales increased 2.5 times as compared to the previous year.[7] In the long-term, it was hoped that the missed calls would begin an interaction which would help in customer engagement and long-term relationship building.

Clearly, dialling and hanging up is no longer a rude, childish game. It means business.

Google

God, an Orwellian Big Brother, Making People Stupid – over the years, Google has been a many-adjectived phenomenon.

Google is probably the first thing we think of when it comes to the Internet.

Baby got green poo? Google it.

Need dad to disinherit brother? Google it.

Want dog to look like donkey? Google it.

So if Google has enjoyed virtually the entire search market in India, why would it need to advertise?

The thing is, search engines do not see themselves as places where-you-type-a-question-and-get-a-zillion-answers. They see search as something that is integral to different things that different people do. Google really did not want you spending time on its site. It might well

[7] Dina, Arzoo, 'How Much Is a Missed Call Worth?', *Livemint*, 13 February 2015

have been the only company which had the objective of reducing the amount of time people spent on its site.

So it was not just Yahoo! and Bing that Google felt the need to stay ahead of. In fact, it was whispered that it perceived Amazon to be a threat – perhaps because that's where a large chunk of the audience headed when searching for products in many markets.

Then there was Facebook, along with whom Google has owned a large part of the mobile-ad market share. And while Facebook and Google are not direct competitors, as a social network, Facebook has been hugely successful in getting referral traffic to other websites like news sites.

Of course, let us not forget the Apple of everyone's eye. While Android and Windows Phone 8 are formidable competitors, Apple has kept up constant pressure with innovations. Plus, Apple's much-touted, ad-blocking support poses a direct threat to the Google way of being.

Then, while many top apps do belong to Google and Facebook, there are also many other apps on which people spend a lot of time. With texting taking over as the new form of talking, texting apps pose a threat too. Most often, search and ads do not suffice as information-givers – people usually ask friends and colleagues questions to validate their choices.

As of mid-2017, Google was processing over 40,000 search queries every second on average which translated to over 3.5 billion searches per day.[8] In fact, way back in 2013, mobile phones had already begun accounting for a lot of traffic when compared to desktops. Google knew it had a sizeable user base on mobiles. It wanted to bring its features to their attention and communicate the many benefits of its products and the Internet.

It also wanted to facilitate usage by weaving stories around innovations. Whatever device people preferred, Google wanted to communicate that it could deliver different things at different times. *And* it also wanted to portray the youth, its largest target audience, as change-makers.

That's how a digital film with a Google-intrinsic story came about.

The film opened in India where an old man named Baldev is seen showing his granddaughter, Suman, an old photograph of two children – himself as a young boy with his childhood friend, Yusuf, in Lahore, in Pakistan. Baldev talks fondly of how the two loved flying kites, stealing sweets from Yusuf's family's sweet shop and hanging out in a park which had an gate so ancient it was from '*Baba Aadam*' times. When Baldev's family left for India after the Partition, the two friends got separated.

It's all Googley-eyed stuff and Google benefits from thereon. Going by the description of the park with the ancient gate in Lahore, the granddaughter searches for

[8] http://www.internetlivestats.com/google-search-statistics/

it on Google – lo and behold, there it is. Having found the gate, she searched for the sweet shop and its number. When she calls up the shop, the call is taken by Yusuf's grandson, who connects her to Yusuf himself. As Suman talks to Yusuf about his old friend, his memories came alive. Next, Yusuf's grandson uses Google to organize his grandfather's visa and check the weather while packing. Then Suman is seen checking the flight time on Google as she heads out to receive them in India. The film ends on an emotional reunion of the two childhood friends, who meet again for the first time in decades.

The film debuted on YouTube in November 2013. It was aired on television a couple of days after that. During the two days in between, the Google film had been viewed more than 1.6 million times on YouTube.

Yes, Google was already the undisputed king with no visible cracks in its armour. So it played on its strengths. The film resonated with people because the Partition has haunted the lives and thoughts of so many. Google took the multi-generational, multi-religion, fratricidal status of India and Pakistan and made itself the happiness-broker, the enabler. The ad also showcased Google as a useful tool with many facets, available not just on computers but also on mobile devices.

The way forward was simple. Taking advantage of the goodwill and the connect people seem to have forged with the two grandfathers and grandchildren, Google India made them feature-ambassadors. It launched a series of smaller ads. In these, in the middle of the grandparents reminiscing or hanging out, a question pops up for which they look to their grandchildren.

The answer, my friend, was not blowing in any wind. It was obviously on Google.

Kindle

When the library moved from that building to the palm of your hand, chances are, you called it a Kindle.

With a huge population that was constantly being exhorted to light the flame of knowledge, India, with its increasing literacy, has long been a market that book publishers could not afford to ignore. The inclination to read was perceived to be high.

But this market for books also reflected the global state of flux – that tug of war that paper and electronic books were indulging in. There were voracious readers. There were time-pass readers, And they all had the potential of being tech-savvy readers – people who could flick a page just by touching it or who could conceivably download a whole reading list on the go.

A vast middle class had spending power, was armed with Internet-enabled devices and the Internet itself had a rapidly expanding reach. Phones were getting smarter and reading apps were easier to access than ever before.

Globally, Amazon's Kindle had been a disruptive force in the existing e-reader market. When it first appeared in

2007, Sony's e-reader, which had been launched earlier, lost market share right away.[9] In India, there was the e-reader Wink and there were other e-readers and ebook apps thinking up new ways to grab attention.

In 2012, Croma became the first retailer in India to offer the latest generation Kindle e-reader from Amazon. Ebook readers had begun making their presence felt – in metropolises like Mumbai, Chennai, Bengaluru, Delhi, Hyderabad and Kochi, as well as in cities like Coimbatore, Bhopal and Vizag.

Many Indians did not own ebook readers because they thought the price was too high. For some, an electronic device, that did more than just read books, made more sense. But in general, if someone had to buy an ebook reader, Kindle would come to mind.

E-readers also had to deal with low consumer-confidence in mobile commerce and in using credit cards online. Though more and more Indians were getting comfortable with online shopping, the same did not reflect when buying ebooks. Books were perceived to be products to be added to a visible, physical collection. There was also the perception that anything electronic like music or a book could be owned by downloading it free off the Internet.

So while the ebook market was projected to be big, it was probably going to take some optimistic years to get there. And some effective campaigns.

---

[9] Bhargava, Shashank, '10 Years of Kindle: What Sells - Ebooks or Physical Ones?', *Hindustan Times*, 19 November 2017

Amazon had managed to create a niche community on Kindle. It presented writers with the opportunity to self-publish, whether they were into fiction, poetry, prose or non-fiction. Amazon allowed them to create an account, upload the book and control pricing. Complete control over the book meant the author could lower the price, run promotions and track sales hourly.

In 2013, the Kindle Direct Publishing (KDP) books accounted for 20 KDP titles on average in the top 100 Kindle list on Amazon in India.[10]

One of the most successful authors in the past decade, Amish Tripathi, initially self-published what was to later become a runaway bestseller (*The Immortals of Meluha*). So who better than Tripathi to be one of the brand ambassadors for Kindle?

The idea was simple.

Take a couple of bestselling authors like Amish Tripathi and Ashwin Sanghi and have them talk about their reading habits. The #CrazyAboutReading campaign was exactly that. In 2015, evocative digital films showed the authors describing personal experiences with Amazon's Kindle and talking about the features they liked. The campaign also leveraged Twitter with a #CrazyAboutReading contest.

From increasing awareness about the Kindle as a device, Amazon India moved on to advertise a flagship product, the Kindle Paperwhite. It aired a three-minute

---

[10] Ganguly, Nivedita, 'The Ebook Story', *The Hindu*, 12 April 2016

TV commercial for the new product. The film followed a young man as he travelled with his Kindle Paperwhite. Journeying by plane, train, bus and boat, he reaches a non-urban area where he is seen reading to a group of excited, eager-looking children. The joy of sharing a story on all their faces said it all.

The biggest challenge for the Kindle involved changing deeply ingrained habits and preferences. But the fact remains that, in 2007, the original Kindle had sold out within hours of its launch in the USA. This hype certainly helped when it came to India as it was already synonymous with ebook readers.

With the most recall value, it faced little competition in India. Other tech product categories saw cutthroat competition but ebook readers were all about Kindle. Sales continued to rise as the market and immediate access to electronic books grew. As far as ebooks went, the category, though tiny, was entirely captured by the Kindle.

At the end of 2016, the sales of Amazon's Kindle e-readers rose 80 per cent to ₹113.28 crore in the year, up to March.[11]

Some features that were intrinsic to the e-reader category also worked in India. Instead of waiting to visit a bookshop, the purchase could be made with one click and you could have the book on the free Kindle Reading app or on your Kindle or iPad in minutes. Wondrous.

---

[11] Shankar, Shashwati, 'Sales of Amazon's Kindle Rose 80% in the Year to March in India', *Economic Times*, 28 December 2016

Electronic books were also tough to lose, and extremely convenient – they were easy to put down and you could pick up where you left off on multiple devices. Browsing for more books was a customized experience because the data on your past reading was helpful in getting suggestions on what else you might like.

Alongside die-hard book romantics who waxed eloquent about the feel of a book, there were equally ardent fans of screens and keys. And even the biggest admirer of books arranged on shelves could not quarrel against the ease with which the same books could be accessed through a small, portable device.

In recent years, though, mobile phones and tablets have overtaken e-readers as reading devices around the world while ebooks themselves have seen a bit of a drop in sales. The sales of physical books have consequently gone up, with 'digital fatigue' being the reason most often quoted for this phenomenon.[12]

Apparently, after all that on-screen time, some people like to stop and smell the pages.

To conclude, companies are forever finding new ways to engage consumers, while innovative products tailored to fit the new marketplace keep getting launched.

---

[12] Milliot, Jim, 'As E-book Sales Decline, Digital Fatigue Grows', *Publishers Weekly*, 17 June 2016

With players like Grofers and Bigbasket, your *kiranewala* has gone dotcom, allowing you to have it all – *sabzi, darzi* and home delivery. Life is in (the) order.

Now not only can you find your *gharwala* (and *gharwali*) online, you can also order the band-*baaja* and *puja* online (with a free video of the rituals, shipping charges extra).

Stores as we knew them are transforming. Chumbak, the quirky lifestyle brand, combines online retail with stores where you can experience the products. Ditto for furniture stores like Pepperfry.

Even *Tinkle*, the decades-old children's magazine, decided to go 'hep' and marry augmented reality with selfie-taking. They made the popular character Suppandi's face a dartboard in their magazine. They also tied up with Blippar so users could download the Blippar app (which enables implementation of AR through image recognition) on their phones and once they pointed it at the dartboard (Suppandi's face), the board came alive on their screens. They could then not only play darts, but they could even take a selfie with Suppandi.

As the market metamorphoses, the marketer has to stay a step or two ahead of the game, gather facts and, therefore, influence people. So when the consumer ventures online, Big Brother-like omnipresent entities are diligently stashing away little factoids – the checking out of ticket prices to Disneyland, then Switzerland and finally Thailand; the purchase of yet another 'Seize the day' nightshirt; the 'occasional' stalking of friends, lovers, peers; and (*shhh*) the visits to porn sites. For the *aam aadmi*, it's now nearly impossible to keep this *Bade Bhaiyya* at bay, unless one chooses to live completely off the grid.

Today, Facebook and Google probably know more about people's other halves than they do – for better or for worse, for richer or for poorer, in sickness and in health – till death do them part (and maybe not even then).

Mining for this kind of gold is not simple though. Between the phones, tablets, laptops, wearables, televisions and what-have-yous being used by people, it is a constantly evolving scenario for marketers.

And since consumers are now considered moving targets (somewhat like animals in the wild), skulduggery may be called for. Keeping an eye on them may involve tracking, geo-targeting, geo-fencing or beacon-ing. They may be fed cookies, evercookies, even supercookies.

Even if they get sick of the cookie diet, the good news (for the *Bade Bhaiyyas*) is that none of those people can really 'check out,' let alone leave (remember-the-death-do-us-part bit?). And, if they do, *Bhaiyya* may just be able to tell everyone what you did last summer.

It's a bummer but all the consumer can do now is occasionally shout when frustrated (with a hashtag): 'Whoisthatguysendinga*fraand*requesttomyMommyon Facebook?'

But it's a new world out there. And Mommy might be the one to turn around and say, 'Just chill, *yaar*.'

Inconclusive

WI-FI, SCI-FI, BHEJA FRY

Will this book be the ultimate brand-aid for you? The evidence is inconclusive (but hey, between you and me, did you really expect any different?).

Marketing, advertising and consumer-ing are as-we-speak evolving in many ways (that being the key takeaway). Doing a random walk-through promises to be an un-illuminating but a good way to conclude.

Evolution has brought up many pressing issues to consider:

Dekh, your Nani's relationship status on Facebook is saying 'single.'

Your four year old is learning an alphabet that goes...R, S, T, U, V, WWW, X, Y, Z.

Your own phone is spying on you.

And that laptop you like working on? (Wait till you hear this.) Imagine getting momentarily distracted from your machine by an ad playing on your television. Now imagine turning back to the computer only to see the same-to-same product category ad on it? Yessir*ji*, your device could be chatting with that TV right under your unsuspecting little nose.

And wasn't there something about televisions with voice-recognition that would not just capture conversations but also upload them for cloud analysis?

Yes, quick, shift that TV out of the bedroom!

But wait, could the refrigerator be listening too?

When sci-fi and wi-fi meet, paranoia can truly make for *bheja* fry. Meanwhile, the joy of getting such detailed dirt on their consumers can make marketers and advertisers cry. After all, this is every marketer's wet dream – one where the consumer is willingly (almost) making the marketer privy to his world.

The consumer is evolving, too, though. Products are being consumed differently from the way they used to be. Why, products themselves can be surprisingly different.

To get their attention, marketers have had to find newer, perhaps more interesting ways. In fact, just when you thought, there was nothing new the world could offer, marketers have found consumer needs that had somehow missed getting discovered before.

Like sexual performance.

Time was when after the deed, partners told each other that the earth had just shaken for them, cuddled and went to sleep.

But, what if they were lying, huh, huh?

There was no reason to worry anymore, though! Getting to the bottom of things has been made easy with a sexual performance app, which measures thrusts and sounds.

As for folks who think cuddling is the better part of sex, why bother with the down-and-dirty part at all? Get the app which finds people in the area to cuddle with – complete with cuddling preferences, ratings and walking directions.

Never before has technology had such immense possibilities.

While the products being offered are getting impressive, communication is finding omni-channels and evolving to new formats – like the gone-in-six-seconds ad.

While some consumers look for a product online only when they find a worm procreating in their chocolate, everyone logs into YouTube to find '*Sheela ki jawaani*'. And while on the quest, they get to see a teeny-tiny commercial just before Sheela arrives.

This six-second ad is so short that before consumers hit 'Skip ad', the ad is over (calling for a high-five among advertisers). This, coupled with the fact that the consumer, especially when on his/her cellphone, has an attention span lower than a monkey in the Delhi Zoo, makes six-seconds pretty much the poster-child for ad durations (for now).

But, contrarily, for every Lightning McQueen of an advertiser, there's also the one who cannot resist telling long-winded stories (sometimes good, sometimes drunken). So more and more brands are also choosing to have long video ads which tell stories. Often screening on a YouTube channel near you, they are marketing's attempt to break free from the clutches of television, its commercials and expensive media spends.

One advantage of the storytelling approach is that it gives consumers a story that will stick in their heads. This makes the plot important, consequently needing time to build up in the film. Though some of these films see a lot of money being pumped in, sometimes the 'digital film' is a euphemism for a cheaply-produced brand commercial with no time constraints. Once unleashed on social media, before you can say h-a-s-h-t-a-g, the film can go viral and see it all – love, hate and emoticonal *atyaachaar*.

The number of views and opinions could be said to be interchangeable with consumer engagement and are, therefore, usually a good return on investment.

Since people are now consuming communication differently on different platforms, speaking to them in a way that interests them has become vital. (Basically, don't speak Tamil to the Greek.) In India, quite a few Internet users are comfortable with regional languages. As more and more consumers are raising their hands (from their devices) to be counted, the language on the said device has taken on a particular significance.

Enter things like Google's language targeting.

But if language helps connect, so do social mores – those customs every great civilization follows. For India, feet-touching-of-everything-older and left-hand-not-touching-anything-edible still count for a lot. But we are nothing if not evolving cosmopolitans, so we've also adopted that universal ritual that binds all humanity – the selfie.

How could we not when it seems to mark every breath between birth and death and some marketing campaigns too? Without doubt, if there is one (still-evolving) social ritual that must be discussed, it is the selfie.

Picture this: A selfie uploaded on a social media site has a caption that reads, 'Looking good, all dressed-up. Feeling sad about the reason why.' It is followed by the tag: #funeral. (Apparently a much-loved Granny has died.)

Even as experts debate this peculiar evolution of sorrow, you could Google 'funeral selfie' and come upon an entire Tumblr page containing selfies at funerals. (Why, even the former US President, Barack Obama succumbed to taking a selfie with European leaders at Nelson Mandela's memorial service. That was not really a funeral, but *still...*)

The selfie itself is not what it used to be. There is now the shoefie, the belfie, the dogfie, the handfie, the reverse selfie and even the felfie. Yes, farmers are taking social media by storm with felfies clicked with farm animals and equipment.

And have you heard of the hijackass? That was the guy who took 'his best selfie ever' with the hijacker of his plane. (Though nitpicky selfie experts pointed out that it wasn't technically a selfie because someone else took the picture.)

So evolved is the selfie that, in 2013, it was crowned the word of the year by the prestigious Oxford English Dictionary.

You could call it self-obssession, narcissism or the end of life as we know it. In the new world, there could just be constantly-connected social media creatures who craft their lives online. In pictures.

As they say, evolution will evolve. The advertiser will just have to look for opportunities to photobomb the consumer's carefully-composed world. (In an acceptable way, of course.) Everything and everyone is evolving.

We will need to keep watching. Because, as that Bollywood movie told us kindly and with prescience, 'Picture *abhi baaki hai, mere dost*.'

Moral(s) of the Story

Rumour has it that advertising is the second most stressful job in the world, right after that of an air traffic controller.

And did you hear about the copywriter in Korea who died of exhaustion at her desk!?

Kasam se, she did.

For the advertising professional exiting office, the world beyond the well, umm...walls of the agency can seem surprisingly confusing. Mere mortals, non-advertising people can startle with their lack of passion.

There's polite interest on their faces when you mention working on a fizzy, carbonated drink. They can yawn when you rave about that ad for cigars you saw on YouTube.

They may actually ask what a Black Book is.

They may not even understand that clever ad you created with the Cannes Awards in mind.

They are different.

Yet, knowing that around 4,551 Parle-G biscuits were consumed every second in 2016 can still turn heads.

You realize that great marketing stories are the classics of the realm. You also realize that you are no longer the clear-headed kid walking wide-eyed into the industry.

Along the way, the lessons in advertising have been fuzzy. Here are a few choice ones, though:

Family (if you have any left) is all that matters. Ogilvy said something to the effect of the customer not being a moron but being your wife/spouse. People forget, I guess, because you'll find ads being created for both.

Brevity is key. To everything. Except when the *lala* of the company (based locally in Patiala or internationally in New York) is giving a speech.

Forget what you may have heard: your client (not his customer) *is* king.

Yes, the lessons are there.

And yes, as we mentioned in the beginning, they are a mix of the real and the farcical. Take the ones you believe.

And Google the rest.

Acknowledgements

Thank you to:

Everyone I have met, or haven't, at Hachette who contributed to this book.

Thomas Abraham, whose idea it was in the first place.

Poulomi Chatterjee, for her savvy inputs.

Prerna Vohra, for her unflappable re-reads.

Priya Singh, in whose capable hands this goes into print, for answering my questions on processes, repeatedly and patiently. And for sparing me her trademark f*** o** b**** look (mostly).

Sandhya Singh, for legal conversations on brands, the Constitution and authors in jail.

My father, the late Maj. Gen. B.P. Singh, who gave me my first book and taught me how to read. And who saw me start out in advertising and who I hope, would have liked to see this.

My mother, Kamala, for her pride and faith in my linguistic abilities ever since I proofread the teacher's note in Grade 2.

My husband, Nagesh, spotter of errors (when asked), whose unexpected calls ('I'm downstairs, want to go to Neemrana for coffee?') rendered many workdays in advertising unproductive but memorable. Ditto in the writing of this book.

And, finally, Avni, my daughter, whose gifts are many, not least being the pink-covered notebook (with matching bookmark) that she made for me. Without that and the numerous glitter-coated pens I stole from her, this book would never, ever have been completed.

Errata

This book has been photographically reproduced from the original text. The following are corrections for typographical errors in the book.

Chapter 2: Ones Upon a Time

p. xxi, line 14, 'Westend Watches' should read 'West End Watch Co.'

Chapter 3: Chaddi Pehan ke Fool Khila Hai

p. 20, line 24, 'In 2016, the total value of the mango drinks market was around ₹6,300 in India.' should read 'In 2016, the total value of the mango drinks market was around ₹6,300 crore in India.'

Chapter 4: Character Loose

p. 58, line 15–16, '"Revealed: The Parle-G girl is Sudha Murthy." "Just revealed: the Parle-G girl is Gunjan Gudaniya."' should read '"Revealed: The Parle-G girl is Sudha Murty." "Just revealed: the Parle-G girl is Gunjan Gundaniya."'

p. 82, line 12, 'ICICI Prudential Bank' should read 'ICICI Prudential Life Insurance Company Limited'

Chapter 7: Badalne Ki Aag

p. 124–5 The paragraph beginning 'In his autobiography...' and the following paragraphs beginning 'The butter bombed in the market...' and 'Amul had to come up with a solution...' and the information in these paragraphs is from Vikram

Doctor, 'How Amul became Utterly Butterly Delicious and Salty', *Economic Times*, 21 July 2007.

p. 128, line 6, 'In FY 2016–17, Amul's sales figures were over ₹27,085 crore in FY 2015–16.' should read 'In FY 2016–17, Amul's sales figures were over ₹27,085 crore.'

p. 136, line 6, 'mega-star Rajniknath's films' should read 'megastar Rajnikanth's films'.

p. 139, line 10, 'In less than a month, the brand got about 1 lakh missed calls from 28,000 numbers.' should read 'In less than a month, the brand received 3.2 lakh missed calls from 28,000 unique numbers.'

Chapter 8: Mummy Badnaam Hui

p. 183, line 10, 'P&G launched Whisper in 1992.' should be 'P&G India launched Whisper in 1989.'

Chapter 9: BTM

p. 200, line 4, 'Maruit Suzuki' should read 'Maruti Suzuki'

p. 208, line 20, 'Mahima Choudhry' should read 'Mahima Chaudhry'

p. 211, line 9, 'Saurav Ganguly' should read 'Sourav Ganguly'

p. 221, line 17, 'If life was a fairy tale, these guys could Also, apparently, most that magic mirror on the wall.' should read 'If life was a fairy tale, these guys could have tried asking that magic mirror on the wall.'